PROJECTS

FOR THE EFL CLASSROOM

RESOURCE MATERIAL FOR TEACHERS

Simon Haines

Nelson

Longman Group Limited
Longman House, Burnt Mill, Harlow,
Essex CM20 2JE, England
and Associated Companies throughout the world.

© Simon Haines   1989

First published by Thomas Nelson and Sons Ltd 1989

This impression Longman Group Ltd. 1995

ISBN 0-17-555736-5

Printed in China
LREX/02

AUTHOR'S ACKNOWLEDGEMENTS

The author wishes to thank the following teachers and
their pupils for their help in piloting and commenting on
the project suggestions contained in this book, and for
contributing their own original project ideas:

Pamela Aboshiha, Steph Dakin, Chris Walton and Sue
Bysh, Concorde International Study Centre, Folkestone,
UK; Lilias Adam, International House, Barcelona, Spain;
Paola Bellodi, Liceo Scientifico, Bologna, Italy; Patricio
Bracamonte and Gustavo Espinoza, Instituto Chileno-
Britanico de Cultura, Santiago, Chile; Stephen Burns,
Gymnase de Chamblandes, Pully, Switzerland; Hugh
Davis, Kensington School of English, London, UK; Maria
Rosina Girotti, ITC Pier Crescenti, Bologna, Italy; Barbara
Kruchin and Phillip Town, Britannia Special English
Studies, Porto Alegre, Brazil; Luisa Fernanda Rodriguez
Lara, IB 'Jose Manuel Caballero Bonald', Jerez de la
Frontera, Spain; Jose Francisco Molina, IB 'Marques de
Comares', Lucena, Spain; Ma Paz Hernandez and Julia
Miquel, IB 'La Asuncion de Na Sa.', Elche, Alicante, Spain;
Jacqueline Moss, Puerto Real, Cadiz, Spain; Helen O'Neill,
British Council, Barcelona, Spain; Marciano Palazzo,
Scuola Media 'Bovio', Foggia, Italy; Carol Perry,
Laboratorio de Idiomas, Alicante, Spain; Maria Carmen
Pinero, Ntra. Sra. de la Caridad, Sanlucar, Spain; Jane
Roux, Deborah Groscoeur and Marion Baron, C.A.R.E.L.,
Université de Poitiers, Royan, France; Yves Saudrais,
Lycée Privé Saint Martin, Rennes, France; Alexandra
Schorah, Barcelona, Spain; Galina Tsekova, English
Language School, Varna, Bulgaria.

ACKNOWLEDGEMENTS

Texts

The publishers wish to thank the following for permission
to reproduce copyright material:

CHAT magazine for the article *Speak up for yourself*
(page 93); The Guardian for the graphs *Percentage of
children who consider themselves to be smokers* (page 90)
and *Deaths on the road* (page 90) and the article *Sex
equality stops at the front door* (page 95); The Hotel Career
Centre, Bournemouth, for the advertisement *Meet people
and travel!* (page 97); J Sainsbury plc for the article
Hyperactivity in children (page 96) from their free leaflet
'Living Today, No. 6 - Facts about food additives'; Schools
Abroad Ltd for extracts from their *Study Plus* brochure
(page 96); Successful Writers Ltd for the advertisement
Learn the secrets of successful writing (page 97); Times
Newspapers Limited for the graph *The great divide: how
we spend our money,* The Sunday Times 6.1.1985 (page 89);
The Vegetarian Society for the article *The price of meat
these days is sheer murder* (page 94).

Every effort has been made to trace owners of copyright,
but if any omissions can be rectified the publishers will be
pleased to make the necessary arrangements.

CONTENTS

CHAPTER 1 INTRODUCTORY NOTES FOR TEACHERS

PROJECTS is a practical resource book which introduces the concept of project work within the context of English language teaching. This introductory chapter defines projects and provides guidelines to help teachers in the preparation and organisation of project work.

Chapter 2 'Resources', suggests ways in which teachers and students can collect and make use of the kinds of resource materials which are necessary for successful project work.

Chapter 3 consists of project ideas which teachers can use with their classes. These are divided into three types:

1 Full Projects
These are detailed stage-by-stage projects which need only a minimum of adaptation by teachers.

2 Project Frameworks
These are less detailed than the Full Projects, so as to allow teachers scope to adapt a topic idea to their particular teaching situation.

3 Further Topic Suggestions
These are very brief thematic outlines which will provide starting points for project work.
(*Note:* One of the major characteristics of this approach to learning is that students themselves should be involved in the basic decisions about the direction and development of topics. In view of this, it is not intended that any of the projects suggested in this book should be followed too closely by teachers and students.)

Chapter 4, 'Case Studies', contains reports from teachers, in different parts of the world, who have used the project work approach with their students. Many of the project ideas and preparatory activities which form the main body of this book have been piloted by these and other teachers.

Chapter 5, 'Lead-in Activities', contains a variety of ready-made practice activities which will help students to prepare for tasks which are common to a wide range of projects. They should be used in connection with specific projects rather than as separate, unrelated language exercises.
(*Note:* All the exercises and activities in this final chapter have been designed to be photocopied and used in the classroom.)

1 WHAT IS PROJECT WORK?

In the context of language learning, projects are multi-skill activities focusing on topics or themes rather than on specific language targets. Of crucial importance is the part which the students themselves play in the initial choice of subject matter and in the decisions related to appropriate working methods, the project timetable and the eventual 'end product'. Because specific language aims are not prescribed, and because students concentrate their efforts and attention on reaching an agreed goal, project work provides students with opportunities to recycle known language and skills in a relatively natural context. Projects can be intensive activities which take place over a short period of time, or extended studies which may take up one or two hours a week for several weeks.

Projects can be divided into four main categories.

1 Information and research projects
Examples:
- The Study of a British Region - page 43.
- English Spoken Here - page 52.
- Pressure Groups - page 53.

2 Survey projects
Examples:
- The British and American Influence on your Way of Life - page 50.
- The Attitudes to your Country of Foreign Visitors- page 47.
- English Language Survey - page 20.

3 Production Projects
Examples:
- News about your Country - page 45.
- Producing a Radio Programme - page 57.
- Class Profile - page 15.

4 Performance and Organisational projects
Examples:
- Organising a British Evening - page 42.
- Starting an English Club - page 51.
- Putting on a Talent Show - page 63.

Project work is not a replacement for other teaching methods, neither is it something which is appropriate only to older or more advanced students. It is primarily an approach to learning which complements mainstream methods and which can be used with almost all levels, ages and abilities of students.

2 THE CHARACTERISTICS OF PROJECT WORK

2.1 Student-centred not syllabus-centred

Once a class embarks on project work, students should become involved in and responsible for all major decisions, especially those related to choice of topic, working methods and the nature of any end product. Students' interest and involvement are essential if they are to be expected to work independently on activities which must be planned and carried out in collaboration with others. This involvement is not incidental to the project but is a crucial and integral part of it. Too frequently language students become over-reliant on coursebooks and examination syllabuses, with their emphasis on controlled practice exercises and artificially contrived tasks. Because project work takes personal interest as its starting point, it allows students to use language more creatively and, by dealing with 'real' subject matter, to increase their knowledge of the world. These can be regarded as 'authentic' rather than purely linguistic objectives.

2.2 Co-operative not competitive

Projects are more likely to succeed if students work co-operatively with others and independently of the teacher towards a mutually agreed goal. The joint end product replaces high marks and teacher approval as the accepted measure of success.

2.3 Skill-based not structure-based

Although at certain stages of most projects, grammatical accuracy is of great importance, only rarely will a particular project lend itself naturally to the systematic practice of specific, predictable language structures. By contrast, most projects, including those outlined in this book, involve a number of related skills. Here is a skill summary of Project 3 (page 25) which clearly demonstrates this variety.

YOUNG PERSON'S GUIDE TO YOUR TOWN

Stage	Skill	Main activities
1	• SPEAKING	class discussion
2	• SPEAKING	group discussion
	• WRITING	making notes
3	• READING	collecting information
	• WRITING	making notes
4	• WRITING	first draft of guide
	• READING	proofreading (correcting written work)
5	• SPEAKING	discussion (decision-making)
	• WRITING	re-writing (final draft of guide)
6	• SPEAKING	reporting back (short talks/class discussion)

(*Note:* Projects which require students to interact in groups or with 'outsiders' may provide opportunities for the practice of specific functional forms.)

2.4 The importance of the end product

A clearly defined and agreed upon end product is an essential feature of project work. Whatever its form, this end product should be the final result of the various tasks students engage in during the project. Without an end product to aim at, projects would have no natural conclusion and activities might become meaningless, unrelated exercises.

Here are a few examples of possible end products:

- a scrapbook collection of writing and pictures
- a formal written report
- a collection of figures or statistics
- a classroom display
- a newspaper
- a student performance
- a radio or video programme

In addition to being a focal point for the whole project, the end product also provides students with an incentive to co-operate with each other, and to present their best work in an attractive form.

3 THE PLACE OF PROJECT WORK IN THE ENGLISH LANGUAGE CURRICULUM

3.1 Coursebooks and project work

A typical English language coursebook, especially at elementary or intermediate levels, might follow a cycle of this kind:

- controlled input of new language (presentation)
- controlled manipulation of new language (practice)
- free language production (transfer)

Whether this cycle takes place during a single lesson or over a number of lessons, it tends to focus on:
- structural forms (grammar)
- communicative forms (functions)
- phonological forms (pronunciation)
- lexical forms (vocabulary)
- skills

However a coursebook syllabus is arranged, its essential purpose is to ensure that students reach prescribed language targets within a specified period of time. Even though students may work independently for short periods, this approach is fundamentally 'authority-centred'. The syllabus determines the content, pace and level; the teacher is the intermediary or agent who 'interprets' the syllabus and presents it to students using an appropriate methodology.

It is at the Transfer stage of this cycle that the central authority of the syllabus is relaxed. Typical activities at this stage may include individual tasks such as writing and reading, or co-operative tasks such as paired dialogues, group discussions, role plays, etc. One of the main aims of these activities is to enable students to choose appropriate language forms for themselves without being over-guided by teachers or textbook prompts. Most teachers would agree that this stage is an essential part of the language-learning process, since it most closely resembles the real world in which students hope eventually to use the language they are learning.

Transfer activities are, however, usually controlled in terms of time, scope, and outcome. Even though precise language forms may not be prescribed, the theme, the approach, and the end product are usually given by the teacher or the coursebook rubric. How often have you gone into a classroom and said:

'Good morning. Today I'd like you to devise your own role play or write a letter.'?

You'd get back the answer:

'A role play about what?' or *'Who shall I write to?'*

Project work may be regarded as a logical extension of Transfer stage activities in that it encourages students to take responsibility for topics, working methods and end products.

3.2 When to do project work

If projects are seen as consolidation or extension activities, it is arguable that they are best placed after a certain amount of a traditional syllabus has been completed. In this situation, a topic raised in a coursebook might provide a suitable starting point for a short, intensive project taking a week's worth of English lessons.

Alternatively, teachers may regard projects as activities which are complementary to the approach dictated by the syllabus. If this is the case, an extended project, taking one or two hours a week for a term, might be more appropriate.
(*Note:* Project work is likely to be taken less seriously as a worthwhile activity if it is used exclusively as an end-of-term 'fun' activity. Irregular attendance, disrupted timetables, and reduced student interest at such times are likely to result in somewhat chaotic and undisciplined projects.)

4 BENEFITS TO STUDENTS

4.1 Contact with reality

Projects provide contacts with real world subject matter which require students to apply and adapt what they already know.

4.2 Projects are participatory activities

Student involvement in making choices and decisions tends to increase their motivation and interest.

4.3 Projects cater for all abilities within a class

Project work enables and encourages students of different abilities to work co-operatively on tasks of equal importance. Those who are relatively weak with regard to their formal linguistic achievement may be able to use other talents which are as valuable to the success of the project as the writing of good English or the understanding of complex texts, etc. Most projects will include some of the following non-linguistic tasks:

- DESIGN — e.g. of leaflets, publicity material, booklets, displays, posters

- ILLUSTRATION — e.g. taking photographs, drawing cartoons, charts, graphs

- ORGANISATION — e.g. of people, materials, tasks and time

- HANDLING EQUIPMENT — e.g. using cameras, cassette or video recorders and typewriters

Students who undertake these tasks will be participating actively in a process which is being conducted through the medium of the English language. This participation may give or restore confidence to less able students and so improve their attitude to language learning in general.

4.4 Projects re-integrate language

For 'normal' teaching purposes foreign languages tend to be broken down into their constituent parts - structures, functions, vocabulary, pronunciation and skills. In such circumstances, projects provide a natural context in which these apparently separate parts can be re-integrated in students' minds. This is crucially important if students are to become confident enough in their own abilities to use English in real situations in the 'outside world'.
(*Note:* The concentration on topics which characterises much project work re-establishes the value of a wide vocabulary. Elsewhere students may regularly be confronted by apparently random lists of new words which they are asked to learn. If they are involved in completing project tasks, students are frequently made aware of the real need to understand and use specific words.)

4.5 Projects establish a context which balances the need for fluency and accuracy

It would be a misunderstanding of the purpose of projects to assume that they are simply opportunities for fluency practice. In most of the projects suggested in this book there are stages in which the need for accuracy will be quite apparent to students themselves. In the proofreading, rewriting and reporting back stages clarity and accuracy of expression are crucial to successful communication. If the end product of a project is a display, a piece of writing, a formal reporting session or a performance, it is in students' own interests to produce language which is both accurate and fluent.

4.6 Projects are a break with routine

This approach to language learning, with its emphasis on interesting topics and student autonomy, and its apparently informal methodology, can in many circumstances provide a welcome break from 'normal' classroom routines. As such it may be seen by students as an antidote to the 'system'. Several of the teachers who took part in the testing of the material in this book claimed that the most important benefit of project work was that it allowed students to relax.

5 TEACHER'S ROLE

The fact that project work is essentially student-centred means that the teacher is no longer in absolute control either of the precise sequence of classroom activities or of language input or output. Before describing the teacher's stage-by-stage role in project work, here are a few general observations.

5.1 Teacher commitment to projects

Perhaps the largest single factor in successful project work is the teacher's belief in and commitment to this method of working. Commitment implies a willingness to adopt a new teaching style. The clear message expressed by those who have experience of projects is that teachers should learn to 'keep out of the way'.

5.2 Teacher's authority

As an authority figure giving up some of your authority, you must be as sure as possible that your students are mature enough to work in this way without feeling cheated, overburdened, confused or leaderless.

Obviously if students misuse the freedom and responsibility on which the success of project work depends, they will not benefit from the activity either from a linguistic or a social point of view. To avoid the possibility of wasted time and effort, teachers should ensure that students are prepared thoroughly before a full project is attempted. Preparation procedures are described in more detail in Section 7 (page 5) of these introductory notes.

5.3 Correcting students' language

While projects are in progress it is essential for students' confidence to be built up. Over-correction of their language in the early stages of a project is likely to inhibit students and to make project tasks seem like any other language exercise. As a matter of routine, students should be expected to proofread each other's written work where this is relevant. During this activity the teacher should act as a reference source alongside dictionaries and grammar books.

If you are unhappy about allowing students' language to go uncorrected, make a discreet note of common mistakes and difficulties. Structural or functional points listed in this way can form the basis of purposeful revision lessons after the completion of the project. See Figure 1 for an example of teacher's notes on language mistakes and difficulties.

Mistakes/difficulties	Context	Students
1 Question forms	Interviews	JS/SF/PT/HR
2 All/most + of	Verbal reports	75% of class
3 Passives	Written summaries	Groups 2 and 5
4 Environment vocabulary	Project topic in general	Whole class

Figure 1

By contrast, 'end product language' should be as accurate as possible. At this stage teachers need have no reservations either about correcting structures which students have been taught and should know, or about helping to make language comprehensible. Indeed students themselves will probably ask for correction, because they will realise that accuracy is important to the communicative effectiveness of their work.

5.4 The teacher's stage-by-stage role

- **Initiating role:**

  Clearly it is for you to decide when project work is appropriate and the length of time it should last. You should then introduce a broad discussion topic which may develop naturally into a project. Once interest is aroused, elicit students' ideas for:

  ▷ the thematic direction of the project
  ▷ methods of working and group formation
  ▷ a project timetable listing a provisional sequence of stages and activities. This will almost certainly need to be adapted as the project develops (see 8.3)
  ▷ a suitable end product

- As soon as this initial phase has been completed, encourage students to think about resource implications. The tracking down of resource material should be regarded as an integral part of the project work process; in other words it is a joint student-teacher responsibility (see Chapter 2). Although it is always useful to have a small collection of resources for students to refer to, teachers should not feel personally responsible for providing all the necessary resources.

- **During the project:**

  Once decisions have been taken and students are engaged in group tasks, you should take on the role of 'facilitator'. This will probably involve you becoming:

  ▷ a source of ideas and advice - being prepared to provide guidance if it is asked for.
  ▷ a referee - helping to resolve arguments or disagreements, especially those about correct language use.
  ▷ chairperson - from time to time groups will report their activities to the whole class. On these occasions the teacher can take on the role of an objective chairperson.

- **Finally:**

  As the project draws to a close, you should become more actively involved in ensuring that the target is reached. Here your functions will be related to efficient organisation:

  ▷ organiser - be actively involved in the organisation of displays, the final production of written reports, etc.
  ▷ evaluator - as well as encouraging students to evaluate the project work process for themselves, you should now be prepared to comment honestly on what students have achieved. (For more detailed notes on the evaluation of projects see Section 10 of these introductory notes.)

6 SUBJECT MATTER/TOPIC

Although, to ensure maximum involvement in projects, students should be encouraged to participate fully in the choice of topics, in practice it may not always be possible to allow students a completely free choice: the teacher should consider resources and other practical implications of any choice made. It is one of your responsibilities therefore to guide students without reducing their interest and enthusiasm. You may, of course, simply impose a single title or present students with a limited choice of titles. Students' involvement will then be restricted to interpreting the titles provided. In certain circumstances, for example where a class finds it impossible to agree amongst themselves, this may be the best way forward. Here are some further points to consider:

6.1 Topics should relate to students' interests and also take account of your teaching circumstances

The nature of project work makes it impossible to predict confidently that particular projects will succeed with particular classes. It is for this reason that the projects outlined in this book should be regarded more as examples which illustrate an approach rather than as rigid reliable blueprints. They should all be adapted to suit your students and your teaching circumstances. Whether a particular topic appeals to a particular class may depend upon some of these factors:
- students' age, sex, background and interests.
- students' previous language learning experiences - clearly, students unused to working independently have more chance of doing a successful first project work if a straightforward topic is chosen.
- students' expectations and needs - your class may be more motivated to work on topics which are directly related to their reasons for learning English. For example, a class of Business English students would probably find Framework Project 6, British or American companies in your country (page 50), of more relevance than Framework Project 5, The Arts in Britain (page 49).

6.2 Topics should take account of location

Certain topics will simply not work if the necessary 'raw material' is unavailable or inaccessible to students. It would, for example, be impossible to attempt Framework Project 4, The Attitudes of Foreign Visitors to your Country (page 00), if you happen to live in a place where foreigners are rarely or never seen.

It is clear, too, that a wider range of topics will be available to students working in a town with an identifiable English-speaking population.

6.3 Start simply

If you or your students have not tried project work before, begin with a topic which is neither too abstract nor too complex. Examples of good 'starter projects' from Chapter 3 include:
- Full Project 1: Class Profile - page 15
- Full Project 3: Young Person's Guide to your Town - page 25

7 PREPARING STUDENTS FOR PROJECT WORK: USING LEAD-IN ACTIVITIES

It could be argued that it is impossible to prepare students for project work if it really is the unpredictable, dynamic learning process of the kind described in these introductory notes. There are, however, certain skills and activities that can usefully be practised before students become involved in a full project. I have called these pre-project tasks 'lead-in activities'.

7.1 Lead-in activities to practise specific skills

Chapter 5 of this book consists of activities which are designed to prepare students for typical project work tasks. See Figure 2 for examples.

Lead-in activity	Relevance to project work
● Giving a short talk	Reporting back/verbal summaries
● Proofreading	Correcting written work/editing
● Writing a questionnaire	Collecting information or opinions
● Conducting an Interview	Collecting information or opinions
● Expressing Information in Different Ways	Processing information
● Making Notes	Recording information efficiently
● Writing Letters	Requesting information/invitations/ making arrangements

Figure 2

If your students regularly do open-ended or extended transfer tasks, they may not need to work through all these lead-in activities.

7.2 Lead-in activities: to practise co-operative working

If students are more used to competing than to working co-operatively with each other, the following groupwork activities may be a useful preparation for the discussions which should form the basis of all decisions concerning the direction and development of project work:
- Coming to an agreement
- Allocating tasks
- Discussing a plan of action

(*Note:* There are some suggestions for Lead-in activities of this kind on page 74.)

7.3 When to do lead-in activities

Each project outlined in Chapter 3 of this book includes suggestions for appropriate lead-in activities. These may be done either before the beginning of the project, or during the project at a time when students realise for themselves that practice in a specific skill is required. Many of the activities listed in 7.1 could be set as homework tasks and would therefore not interfere directly with the smooth running of the project.

8 ORGANISING PROJECT WORK

8.1 Getting started

Once you are confident that students are capable of working co-operatively in groups and without constant teacher control, prepare for a project.

Over-detailed plans at this stage will reduce the value of the project as a participatory activity, so restrict your planning to the following:

- decide on a broad theme to propose to the class.
- devise a way of introducing this theme in an interesting, thought-provoking way. Here are a few examples of introductions suggested in connection with the Full and Framework Projects in Chapter 3:

  ▷ give the class a genuine reason for undertaking a particular project.

  ▷ show a video which raises appropriate issues.

  ▷ play a pop record.

  ▷ involve students personally by means of a class survey or a quiz.

- collect together a few introductory resources which may be used in the early stages of groupwork.

8.2 Timing

Projects may last a day, a week, a month or longer. If you decide that your students can afford to spend, for example, six hours on project work, you may distribute this time in a number of ways:

- 1 hour a week for 6 weeks, • 2 hours a week for 3 weeks,
- 3 hours a week for 2 weeks, • 6 consecutive hours.

(*Note:* Start modestly and gradually build up to longer, more ambitious projects.)

Although you may need to set an overall time limit and fix a completion date, try to remain flexible within this. In other words, do not commit yourself to precise lengths of time for each of the stages and, if possible, allow different groups to spend varying lengths of time over particular activities or stages. Some tasks, for example conducting opinion surveys, may take longer than either you or your students anticipate. In many cases the dynamism of the project will alter timings. As a general rule, the larger the class, the longer each stage will take.

8.3 Project timetable

Once initial class discussion has produced content ideas, agreed objectives and suggested working methods, a preliminary project timetable can be drawn up. This should outline the main activities and groupings as well as the intended outcomes for each stage. The timetable should always be regarded as a flexible programme which records and reminds students of the suggestions and decisions that were made during the opening class discussion.

Figure 3 is an example of a provisional timetable for the English Language Survey project which is described fully on page 20.

SAMPLE PROJECT TIMETABLE

Project Title: English Language Survey
Time Available: 6 - 10½ hours

Stage	Main activities	Student groupings	Location	Outcomes
1	• Class discussion	Whole class	Class	• Decision on scope and content of project
2	• Discussion	Small groups	Class	• Plan of campaign • Allocation of tasks
3	• Writing	Individuals/Pairs	Class/Home	• Survey questions
4	• Interviewing	Individuals/Pairs	Home/school/town	• Collection of information
5	• Processing information	Groups/Pairs or individuals	Class/home	• Summaries of information
6	• Checking/ proofreading • Rewriting	Individuals/Pairs	Class	• Corrected summaries of Stage 5 writing
7	• Display • Reporting back • Discussion	Groups Whole class	Class	 • Verbal reports • Survey conclusions

Figure 3

8.4 Location

A majority of project work tasks can be done successfully in the classroom. However, there are certain tasks, particularly information-gathering activities, for which students will need to consult reference sources, visit particular places or talk to 'outsiders' (e.g. members of the public) either in other parts of the school or entirely outside the school. If it is impossible, for whatever reason, in your teaching situation to allow students out of the classroom during teaching time, try to arrange for these tasks to be done in students' own time (e.g. for homework). Figure 4 summarises the location possibilities for a variety of project activities.

(*Note:* Several teachers have reported that student groups meet in cafes or bars to continue project work outside school time.)

8.5 Student groupings

At different stages of project work students can expect to work in different combinations. I would suggest that all projects start and end with whole class discussions. During the various in-between stages students should work in groups of 4-6. However, within this basic grouping not all tasks will involve whole groups. Many tasks are best done by individuals or pairs.

In general it is best to allow students to form their own groups and pairs, on the basis either of specific interests or of friendship. There will, of course, be circumstances in which you would prefer not to allow certain combinations of students to work together; you should deal with this in your usual way.

Remember that because project work is essentially a co-operative learning method, you should always allow sufficient time for purposeful, structured discussions and reporting back sessions. As a matter of course, individuals should report to the whole class at certain times during the project. This reminds students that they are involved in a whole class activity.

9 PROBLEMS

Although a majority of language teachers are attracted to the idea of project work and agree with the educational aims of this approach to learning, many are apprehensive about difficulties associated with project organisation and student discipline.

9.1 General guidelines

- Reconsider the potential benefits of project work:
  ▷ students work co-operatively and independently of the teacher.
  ▷ projects are a break from routine.
  ▷ students engage in authentic activities aimed at an end product.
  ▷ projects provide fluency practice.
  ▷ students use a variety of language skills in natural combinations.
  ▷ projects can help build students' confidence.

Do these benefits outweigh potential problems associated with projects?

- Prepare your students for project work. Prior to starting a 'real' project give them practice in working independently in groups for increasingly long periods of time.
- Build up a stock of accessible resources (see Chapter 2, page 11).
- Start with short, uncomplicated projects.

9.2 Specific problems

1 Students lack interest or motivation

- Lack of sustained interest may be due simply to students' immaturity. If your students are incapable of working independently despite all your preparations, abandon project work until a later date. The gap between project work and your 'normal' way of teaching may be so great that students need more time to adjust psychologically to the idea of projects.

Activity	Ideal location	Alternatives
● Group or class discussions	Classroom	None
● Background reading research, etc.	Library	Classroom + resources Home/local library in own time
● Writing: individuals	Home	Classroom
● Writing: pairs/groups	Classroom	None
● Interviews with public	Town/community	Home/own time
● Taking photographs	Outside	Home/own time/find ready-made photos
● Studying places	Outside	Home/own time/use maps
● Reporting back/displays	Classroom	None

Figure 4

This problem may be particularly characteristic of a class of adult students who are used to, prefer and expect a directive approach to teaching.

- You may have been over-directive and not allowed students to participate enough in the initial decision-making processes.
- The project may be taking too long. Try a whole class discussion to redirect the project so that the conclusion is reached more quickly.
- This may be an intrinsically uninteresting topic. If so, the teacher must decide whether it is worth continuing at all. It might be better to stop the project and start with a new idea at a later date.

2 A few students disrupt otherwise successful project work:

- Distribute potentially difficult students among the various working groups.
- Encourage students to make use of all their talents. Even those who are poor at English may have other skills which could be useful to the work of their group (organisation, equipment handling, design, illustration, photography, etc.). Make sure that other students are aware of the value of such skills. A troublesome minority cannot be allowed to ruin an otherwise successful activity. If certain students are determined not to co-operate, give them more traditional language learning activities for the periods when the rest of the class is involved in project work.

3 Students speak in their own language instead of using English

It is idealistic to expect elementary and lower intermediate students to work in English throughout a project. Once they become absorbed in a topic, or as soon as they are outside the classroom, they will almost certainly lapse into their own language. Without resorting to authoritarian measures or threats, there is nothing you can do about this. Why not make a deal with students? Allow them to conduct certain organisational and planning discussions in their own language, but insist that they speak English for topic discussion, reporting back sessions, short talks and whole class discussions.

4 You are worried about the number of language mistakes made by students

Remember that one of the main aims of project work is to build students' confidence.

Try to establish in their minds that on certain occasions grammatical accuracy is important: e.g. in written work and when reporting back, whereas on other occasions complete accuracy is less important than interest, involvement and communication. You should be able to achieve this understanding by a convincing initial explanation followed by a consistent policy of correcting or ignoring language errors.

5 Students do not regard projects as 'real' work:

- It is quite possible that some students will question the value of project work. If they have come to see learning English primarily as a means of passing examinations and getting a good job, the time spent on informal project work may seem insufficiently focused to be of real value. If it seems likely that more than a small minority of your class will react in this way, spend some time explaining the purposes and benefits of projects. Also point out that you will be monitoring their discussions and assessing their written work just as you would in the case of more formal language learning exercises.
- You may decide to do formal follow-up language work after each project session, or you may leave this kind of remedial activity until the end of the project.
- If this is a serious problem with your class, intersperse project work sessions with the kind of work students regard as purposeful. If, for example, your class has five hours of English a week, use only one or two of these hours for project work. It may be possible to relate more formal language lessons directly to project work.

6 You cannot let your students do project work outside the classroom

While it is a great advantage to be able to send students out of the classroom in pairs or small groups to do project assignments, it is not the end of the world if for some reason this is impossible. Many of the projects outlined in this book can be done quite adequately by a combination of classwork and homework. (See 8.4 Location, page 7.)

7 Groups work at different speeds

- Suggest extension activities to groups who finish early.
- Students in the fastest group could take on an organisational responsibility by helping slower groups, or by becoming 'reporters' or 'co-ordinators' for the whole project.

10 RECORD KEEPING AND PROJECT EVALUATION

It is quite possible to regard project work as valuable for its own sake. In some teachers' minds an activity which motivates and interests students, and which promotes self-confidence, class cohesion and co-operative working towards an authentic end product, may need no further justification. Many teachers, however, think it is important to keep a record of what their students achieve and to be in a position to evaluate the effectiveness of a project as objectively as possible.

10.1 During the project

- Monitoring by the teacher:
  Discreet monitoring of student tasks should enable the teacher to:
  ▷ assess what students are learning.
  ▷ make a note of language mistakes and decide which points need remedial attention.
  ▷ check that students are working well together in pairs or groups.

● Recording progress:
  ▷ If project work is done only intermittently, for example for one hour a week, suggest that groups keep their own record of what they have done in each session. See Figure 5 for an example.

Group A

Monday 5th Oct   1   Discussion to plan collection of information: Jose will find out about travel costs. Maria will write a letter requesting information about holidays in Scotland.

                     2   Problems: not enough time/we couldn't find the address of the Scottish Tourist Board.

Monday 12th Oct

Figure 5

This kind of 'project diary' will be useful to students themselves during the project, and may help the teacher to evaluate the whole process after the completion of the project.
  ▷ the teacher should also note the progress and achievement of the class, session by session. See Figure 6 for an example.

10.2 After the project

Unlike many other learning activities, projects cannot be marked objectively. Of course students may be graded according to their degree of effort or involvement, individual pieces of written work may be marked, and verbal reports can be assessed. However, most teachers will want to know whether and how individuals have benefited from doing project work, and whether the process as a whole has been successful. Clearly, if students are working co-operatively in groups to produce a joint piece of work, success cannot be measured solely by the traditionally practised methods. Here are some suggestions for ways of evaluating the overall effectiveness of a project:

● By referring to the notes made during project work, the teacher could write lists of 'plus' and 'minus' points. See Figure 7 for an example.

Date	Group	Stage	Notes: achievements, successes, failures
5th Oct	A	2	Interesting discussion: all students took part. Problem: incomplete planning notes.
	B	2	Allocation of individual tasks took too long. Students could not agree on who should do what.
	C	3	Fastest group: short effective discussion. Students are now collecting information.
12th Oct			

Figure 6

Plus	**Minus**
1 Students spoke more English than in 'normal' English lessons.	1 Not all groups spoke English all the time.
2 Elena and Ana gained in self confidence.	2 Written work contained too many simple mistakes.
3 Jose showed himself to be a capable organiser.	3 Three or four students did hardly any work.
4 Students practised and mastered polite request forms.	4 This project needed a lot of extra preparation by the teacher.
5 Most students practised letter-writing skills.	5 Difficult to find appropriate resources at the right level.
6 Students learnt a lot of new vocabulary.	

Figure 7

• Devise a questionnaire to help assess the value of the project. See Figure 8 for an example:

• Discuss the project with the class. Points to talk about:
1 Did students enjoy the project?
2 What did they learn: new language/skills/information?
3 Which activities did students find most useful/most enjoyable/most pointless, etc?
4 What can students do in English now that they could not do before?

Taking all this information into account, teachers should now weigh up the advantages and disadvantages of the project, and finally ask themselves the question: 'Was this project worth doing?'

---

1 How interested were the students in the topic?
Very   Quite   Not at all

2 How many of the six groups worked well together?
1   2   3   4   5   6

3 How much time was wasted?
a lot   a little   none

4 Did students accept this as a valid way of learning?
Yes   No

5 Are you satisfied with your role in the project?
Yes   No

6 How could the project have been improved?

Figure 8

CHAPTER 2 / RESOURCES

Unfortunately a book of this kind cannot predict with certainty which projects will succeed with your classes. As I have emphasised in the introductory notes in Chapter 1, teacher commitment and student involvement are crucial. An equally important factor is the availability of a range of resources. While it would be highly desirable for all teachers to keep a permanent 'English Department' stock of project resources, in many teaching situations it would be impossible to build up such a collection overnight. Quite apart from this practical difficulty, teachers should make a deliberate policy of encouraging students to regard the tracking down and collecting of resources as an integral part of their involvement in project work. This basic skill is an authentic research activity and should not be seen as the responsibility solely of the teacher.

Whether you are considering starting a resource bank, or simply wish to prepare yourself for a particular project, here are a few suggestions about the kinds of resources to collect and how to collect them.

WHAT TO COLLECT (1): PRINTED MATERIALS

Many teachers will already be used to cutting out interesting newspaper articles and keeping them for possible future use. This process should be extended systematically to include the collection of all kinds of printed matter, including:

- newspapers, magazines, books, tourist brochures, maps, advertisements, etc.
- information packs produced by business organisations, charities, embassies, tourist offices, airlines, banks, hotels, shops.

(*Note:* You may continue to select and cut out interesting texts, but if storage space is not a problem, it is probably advisable to keep whole publications in their original forms.)

WHAT TO COLLECT (2): RECORDED MATERIALS

A collection of recorded materials can also be useful as a project work resource available to students, although, clearly, this will take more time and effort to build up. Here are a few ideas:

- cassette recordings of English-language radio programmes (e.g. BBC World Service), including documentaries on specific topics, news programmes, information about Britain and other English-speaking countries, profiles of internationally known personalities.
- current pop songs in which interesting issues are raised. Teachers might usefully ask students for their assistance in selecting and recording such a collection.
- video recordings of TV programmes about life in Britain and documentaries on specific themes of international importance. Pre-recorded video cassettes: feature films, documentaries, etc.

(*Note:* Making an extensive collection of video cassettes may well be beyond the financial means of many English language departments or schools. If this is the case, a practical alternative would be to hire or borrow videos and films from commercial agencies or film libraries.)

WHAT TO COLLECT (3): AUTHENTIC EXAMPLES

It is useful to keep a small collection of authentic examples of the kinds of materials students themselves are asked to produce during projects. It is the format, wording, style and design of these examples that will be especiallly useful to students. Such materials might include:

- letters of various kinds: e.g. requesting information, arranging visits, thanking someone for help, inviting someone to take part in a function or event.
- questionnaires, quizzes, opinion surveys - these are often found in magazines or newspapers.
- recordings from radio and television of interviews, short talks, discussions, news reports, etc.

REFERENCE MATERIALS

The kinds of resource listed above could be regarded as either disposable or for reference. You should also, however, consider extending or building up your stock of permanent reference books. This might include:

- dictionaries of various kinds, e.g. bi-lingual, English-English, specialist vocabulary areas such as Business English, etc,
- grammar reference books at students' level,
- reading and writing skills books,
- encyclopaedias both in the students' own language and in English,
- books about Britain, the USA, etc.

WHERE TO FIND RESOURCES (1): PERSONAL CONTACTS

- Resources or information on particular topics may be requested from teachers' or pupils' contacts abroad. Contacts might include: a school abroad with which your school has an exchange; a town with which your own town is twinned; an individual (penfriend) or group correspondence link; personal friends or relatives of teachers or students.
  (*Note:* Getting students to write letters asking for information and resources could be turned into an extended project in its own right.)
- English-speaking residents of your country (permanent or temporary) might be prepared to provide you with information or resources. If you are in contact with Britons or Americans living in your town, why not ask them to let you have any newspapers or magazines, etc. when they have finished with them. Such residents might include: business people, teachers, elderly retired people, visiting students, etc.
  (*Note:* Keep a list of the names and addresses of individuals who would be willing to provide resources, give talks, answer students' questions, take part in surveys, etc.)

WHERE TO FIND RESOURCES (2): AGENCIES IN YOUR COUNTRY

- your own school, town, region: business organisations, banks, other language schools, tourist agencies, stations, airports, etc.
- your nearest university: the English and other Departments
- libraries, museums, exhibition centres, etc.
- institutions concerned with English-speaking countries, e.g. the American Embassy, the British Council, etc.

WHERE TO FIND RESOURCES (3): OFFICIAL INFORMATION SOURCES IN ENGLISH-SPEAKING COUNTRIES

- tourist boards*
- international charity organisations (e.g. Oxfam)
- international pressure groups (e.g. Greenpeace or Friends of the Earth)
- your country's embassies in UK, USA, Australia, etc.
- * See Appendix on page 108 for the addresses of British Regional Tourist Boards.

EQUIPMENT (1): THE BASICS

There are certain very basic items of equipment which will be needed by students at various stages of project work. Without these, students will find difficulty in producing a high quality of presentation:

- pens, pencils, paper, rulers, scissors, glue, colouring pens, files, notepads, clip-boards, display space (e.g. classroom walls).

- cassette recorders: these might not be appropriate for all projects, but could be a very convenient way of recording interviews, short talks, etc. The recorded material could be transcribed, summarised, discussed or otherwise exploited in the classroom at a later stage in the project.

EQUIPMENT (2): EXTRAS

More ambitious students will find these extra items of equipment of value in producing more professional-looking work:

- **a photocopier**
  Many teachers now depend on photocopiers to produce their own teaching materials. If it is possible to allow students limited access to the school or department photocopier, this will save them time at the information-collecting stage of projects, and help them to produce more professional and elegant end product material.

- **cameras** (35mm, 'Instamatic' or polaroid)
  Certain projects, for example Full Project 3: Young Person's Guide to Your Town (page 00), will benefit greatly from the inclusion of photographs taken and selected by students themselves. Original illustrations are often preferable to those 'lifted' from existing publications.
  (*Note:* The local photographic society or the school camera club may be prepared to develop your students' films free of charge.)

- **a video camera**
  From the students' point of view, a video camera would open up a completely new dimension to project work. You may consider, however, that training students to use sophisticated equipment like this would take an unjustifiable length of time in relation to its value as part of a language-learning activity.
  Teachers, however, might want to consider making video recordings of their students working on project tasks, for example conducting street interviews, or taking part in group discussions. Such recordings could be very useful at the project evaluation stage.
  (*Note:* An example of a video project is described on page 62.)

- **a typewriter or word processor**
  These items of equipment would enable students to produce more professional-looking writtten work. Word processors are particularly useful for purposes of editing, correcting or reordering written texts. Again, however, teachers will have to decide whether using such equipment is relevant to the main aims of project work.

(*Note:* Many of the items of equipment listed above are sophisticated and expensive, and might not be easily available to most teachers. They are mentioned here only as refinements and are in no way necessary or essential to the success of the process of project work. Some of the students themselves may have personal access to these items of equipment. Only encourage them to use these if it is not likely to cause resentment in other students.)

PROJECT RESOURCES

Aim: To start a resource collection to support student projects.

Participants: A group of teachers from one or more schools

and/or: A group of advanced students of English

Stage	Main activity	Purposes and details of activity
1	• Whole group discussion	• Discuss what sort of a resource collection you want. • Discuss the criteria for selecting material, e.g. level of English, length, specific topics. • Form working groups and allocate group responsibilities. Examples: Group A: recorded material – video and audio. Group B: printed materials – newspapers and magazines. Group C: printed materials – books. Group D: establish useful contacts and compile a list of information sources in and beyond the local community.
2	• Small group discussions	• Allocate tasks to individuals or pairs within groups. Examples: Group A: 1 video. 2 audio – radio. 3 audio – songs. Group B: 1 newspapers. 2 magazines.
3	• Information collection	• Individuals/pairs start collecting. *(This stage could last one day or be continued for several days or weeks.)*
4	• Reporting back • Group evaluation	• Individuals/pairs bring in material and information collected to show to their group. • Group examines and assesses value of resources collected in the light of criteria discussed in Stage 1.
5	• Whole group discussion	• Group discusses how best to classify and store resources, and how to keep the collection up-to-date. • Form working groups and allocate responsibilities. Examples: Group A: resource classification. Group B: storage. Group C: access by teachers/students. Group D: method of up-dating and adding to collection.
6	• Group discussion	• Formulate plans: Examples: Group A: decide whether to classify resources by topic, level or type (e.g. cassette/print) Group B: decide where collection should be kept (e.g. classroom, library) and how material should be stored (e.g. filing cabinet, boxes on shelves).
7	• Reporting back • Whole group discussion	• Groups report ideas. • Whole group makes collective decisions and then works out method of using the resource collection. • Write guidelines for users.

Figure 9

NOTES ON COLLECTING AND STORING RESOURCES

- Involve a group of people in collecting materials: students and other teachers at your school would be ideal 'helpers'.
- Initially collect anything and everything. You don't know when certain items may be useful. Try to ensure a steady supply of new materials.
- A large three- or four-drawer metal filing cabinet, with separate hanging folders, is ideal for the storage of individual articles or texts. Much more space is needed if you intend to collect whole publications such as newspapers or magazines.
- Devise a method of classifying and coding resources collected. Start by classifying and filing materials by theme. Typical themes might include:
  - Art
  - Clothes and Fashion
  - Crime
  - The Environment
  - Families
  - Festivals and Celebrations
  - Food and Drink
  - History
  - Houses and Homes
  - Politics
  - Regions of Britain
- A further sophistication would be to 'rough-grade' resources (using coloured labels) on the basis of their suitability for elementary, intermediate or advanced students.
- If you have a computer or word processor at your disposal (and plenty of time!), you could keep an up-to-date list of the articles in your files.

RESOURCE COLLECTION PROJECT (FOR TEACHERS AND/OR ADVANCED STUDENTS)

Larger language schools may be lucky enough to have a member of staff responsible for resource management. Teachers who do not have this facility and who are used to finding their own resources, might consider collaborating in groups on a Resource Collection Project. Advanced students might also be asked to help. Figure 9 is a suggested outline.

FULL PROJECTS

1 CLASS PROFILE

1 Suitability

Level .... All levels
Age: .... All ages
Class: .... Students who have recently
come together as a class

**Approximate
time:** .... 4 – 10 hours

2 Project description

This is a good 'starter', suitable for teachers and students unfamiliar with project work. The subject matter, relevant to most learning situations, is especially suitable for groups of students who do not already know each other well, or for elementary classes who have recently learnt the language of asking for and giving personal information and of personal descriptions.

Because the students themselves are the basic 'raw material', this project should be simple to introduce, resource and organise. The only essential prerequisite is that your students should have an interest in finding out about each other.

3 Variations

● Students write about themselves instead of about each other.
● The main emphasis is on the class as a whole rather than on individuals.
● The project is orientated towards a business or company rather than a school. (This might be appropriate in situations where students feel no school loyalty.)

4 End product

Format: Classroom display and/or scrapbook containing:
● Written descriptions, family trees, anecdotes
● Illustrations: photographs, drawings, cartoons, plans, etc.
● Interviews: on cassette or in writing

Contents: ● Profiles of students in the class, including: physical descriptions; families; jobs, hobbies and interests; past experiences; future ambitions; attitudes and opinions.
● Possible extensions: teacher profiles; lessons/teaching methods; classroom/school

5 Summary of stages

Stage	Main activities	Outcome	Time (hours)
1 Basic	Discussion	Idea of project scope	½ – 1
2 Basic	Writing/Interviewing	Information for profiles	1
3 Basic	Writing/Proofreading	Written profiles	1½
4 Extension*	Discussion	Plans for extra sections	½
5 Extension	Research/Writing	Draft form of extras	1 – 1½
6 Extension	Proofreading/Rewriting	Final form of extras	1
7 Basic	Reporting/Discussion	Display/Presentations	1 – 2
8 Extension	Discussion/Production	Finished scrapbook	1 – 1½
		Total Basic stages	4 – 5½
		Total (Basic + Extension)	7 – 10

Note: Only do Extension stages if you are sure students' interest will be maintained.

6 Resources

Essential: ● Normal stationery equipment: pens, paper, etc.
● Existing photographs
Additional: ● A cassette recorder for interviews
● A camera to enable students to take specific photographs

7 Location

Basic stages – the classroom   **Extension stages** – other areas of the school
Clearly, individual written work may be done elsewhere – e.g. for homework.

8 Lead-in Activities

9 **Stage-by-stage guide**

Stage 1 – Introduction (basic)

Aim:	To arouse student interest in this project	**Approximate time:**
Main activity:	Class discussion	**½ –1 hour**
Intended outcomes:	1 A clear idea of the scope of the project	
	2 The formation of student pairs	

ACTIVITIES

Teacher   **Students**

1 Arouse interest in Class Profile, Suggestions:
   • Demonstrate how little students really know about each other.
   • Get students to find out five facts about another member of the class.
   • Explain that another class in the school is interested in getting to know your students.
   • Tell students they will be involved in an exchange of information with a class in another school (in your country or in the UK).

2 Ask students for suggestions for possible contents of a Class Profile. Note ideas on the board and then discuss each in turn. Examples:

Suggest content ideas.
Discuss ideas more fully.
Express opinions and make decisions.

   • Profiles of individual students. What form might these take? (Written descriptions/short talks, etc.). How would they best be produced? (By each student about him/herself or by students about each other?)
   • Profiles of teachers. Which teachers?
   • Descriptions of lessons/teaching methods/classroom/school.

3 Once scope of project has been established, students form pairs in preparation for Stage 2.

Choose working partners.

Stage 2 (basic)

Main activities:	Discussion/Writing/Interviews	**Approximate time:**
Lead-in activity:	Writing a questionnaire - page 84	**1 hour**
Intended outcome:	Information necessary for producing student profiles	

ACTIVITIES

Students   **Teacher**
(In pairs formed in Stage 1)

1 Discuss what information they want to form the basis of an individual profile of other students. Examples:

Explain this stage. Monitor initial discussions.

   • Facts: age, physical description, job, family.
   • Interests: sports, hobbies.
   • Past experiences and future plans.
   • Attitudes and opinions.

2 Decide how to collect this information. Examples:

Monitor.

   • Interview • Written questionnaire

3 Write interview or questionnaire questions.

Check questions.

4 Each pair of students finds another pair to question. Method:
Interviews - Student A interviews Student C, while Student B notes C's answers, etc.
Questionnaires - Students exchange and fill in written questionnaires.

Monitor, but help only where there is breakdown in communication.

Stage 3 (basic)

Main activities: Writing/Proofreading
Lead-in activity: Proofreading (page 81)
Intended outcome: Corrected written profiles of students

Approximate time: 1½ hours

ACTIVITIES

Students	Teacher
	Explain this stage.
1 Using notes written during interviews or answers to written questionnaires, each student writes the first draft of a description of another class member. (Homework exercise?)	Monitor first draft writing. Do not correct but give help with vocabulary.
2 Students exchange written descriptions and proofread the description of themselves. Students check writing for language mistakes and errors of fact.	
3 Return corrected description to writer, and discuss changes or improvements	Monitor discussions and help resolve disagreements about correct language.
4 Students re-write descriptions incorporating agreed changes.	

(*Note:* If students are interested in continuing this project go on to Extension Stages 4-6. If not, move directly on to Stage 7.)

Stage 4 (extension)

Main activity: Class discussion
Intended outcomes: 1 Plans for additional sections of project
2 Formation of new working groups

Approximate time: ½ hour

ACTIVITIES

Students	Teacher
1 Make final decisions about additional topics to include in Class Profile. Examples: ● Profiles of teacher(s) ● (English) lessons ● Classroom (atmosphere) ● School life	Remind students of suggestions made during initial Stage 1 discussion.
2 Form interest groups (maximum four students)* to work on one of these topics. Examples: ● Group A decides to produce profile of teachers. ● Group B decides to describe school life, etc.	Oversee group formation.

*More than one group may work on the same topic.

Stage 5 (extension)

Main activities: Discussion/Research/Writing
Intended outcome: Draft versions of additional section

Approximate time:
1–1½ hours

ACTIVITIES

Students	Teacher
(Working in the new groups)	
1 Groups plan chosen section and allocate tasks. Examples:	Explain this stage.
• Group A (Teacher Profiles) may decide that one pair of students should interview an English teacher, while the other pair should write brief descriptions of teachers of other subjects. Alternatively, an artist in the group might produce sketches of teachers.	Make rules clear: Can students go out of the classroom to interview teachers, check layout of the school, etc?
• Group B (School Life) may decide to allocate tasks to individual students: Student 1: draw and label plan of school Student 2: take photographs Student 3: produce an advertisement for the school Student 4: interview other students to produce report on students' impressions of school life	Monitor discussions
2 Follow procedure outlined in Stages 2 and 3. • Collect information • Write up in draft form	Remind students of this procedure.

Stage 6 (extension)

Main activities: Proofreading/Rewriting
Intended outcome: Final versions of remaining project sections

Approximate time:
1 hour

ACTIVITIES

Students	Teacher
1 Exchange work produced in Stage 5 with another member of group.	Remind students about the idea of proofreading.
2 Read and correct written work, comment on ideas and question partners about content.	Monitor correcting task, intervening only in cases of disagreement.
3 Rewrite work, incorporating agreed corrections and improvements.	Remind students that clarity and accuracy are important at this stage.

Stage 7 (basic)

Main activities: Reporting back/Discussion
Lead-in activity: Giving a short talk (page 79)
Intended outcomes: 1 Classroom display of all work produced
2 Class awareness of project content

Approximate time:
1 – 2 hours

ACTIVITIES

Students

1 Display all material from Stage 3 on classroom walls or on desks.

2 Students give short talk, lasting a minute, about the class member they described.
3 Display all material from Stage 6.
4 Group representatives describe in turn what their group has been doing.
5 Students ask questions and comment on each other's work.

Teacher

Explain this stage.
Help to organise displays and presentations.

Allow time for the preparation of talks.

Participate in the questioning and commenting activity.

Stage 8 (extension)

Main activities: Discussion/Production
Intended outcome: Finished scrapbook

Approximate time:
1 – 1½ hours

ACTIVITIES

Students
1 Discuss format, appearance and length of scrapbook.
2 Form new working groups to edit and re-order material to fit agreed format.
3 Put material together into scrapbook form

Teacher
Participate in discussion.

Give practical help.

2 ENGLISH LANGUAGE SURVEY

1 Suitability

Level .... Intermediate/Advanced
Age: .... Secondary/Young adults
Class: .... Students should be mature or reliable enough to work independently outside the classroom, without constant teacher supervision
Situation: .... This project is intended for classes studying in their own countries. If you are working in an English-speaking country, see Variations.

Approximate time: .... 6–11 hours

2 Project description

This is a 'survey' project in which students investigate the extent to which ordinary people in their town know English. Students should plan the details of their investigations in the classroom and then go out into the streets of their town to interview members of the public. While it would be unnatural to expect whole interviews to be conducted in English, especially if those being interviewed know little or no English, students should be encouraged to use English with any competent speakers they meet. The length of time this project takes will clearly depend on the number of people interviewed and on the number of questions asked. (This accounts for the difference between the minimum and maximum times given.)

3 Variations

- Classes studying in Britain could interview British people about their knowledge of foreign languages.
- In situations where it is impractical to allow students to conduct street interviews, information could be collected from relatives and friends in students' own time.
- Instead of asking interviewees about their personal knowledge of English, students could ask questions about people's attitudes to the importance of knowing English in the modern world.

4 End product

Format: Report containing:
  - Charts, completed questionnaires, statistics
  - Interviews: on cassette or in writing
Contents: - The results of an investigation (survey) into the extent to which people of students' own nationality know English.

5 Summary of stages

Stage	Main activities	Outcome	Time (hours)
1	Class discussion	Idea of scope of project	$\frac{1}{2}$–1
2	Group discussions	Plans/Task allocation	$\frac{1}{2}$
3	Writing	Survey questions	1
4	Interviewing	Collection of data	1–3
5	Processing of information	Summaries of data collected	1–3
6	Proofreading/Rewriting	Corrected data summaries	1
7	Reporting/Discussion	Survey conclusions	1
		Total anticipated time	6–10$\frac{1}{2}$ hours

6 Resources

Essential: - Pens, paper, clip-boards
  - People willing to be interviewed
Additional: - A cassette recorder for interviews

7 Location

- Stages 1, 2, 3, 6, 7 – the classroom.
- Stage 4 – streets, cafes, parks, stations, etc.
- Stage 5 – classroom or home.

8 Lead-in activities

9   **Stage-by-stage guide**

Stage 1 – Introduction

Aim: To arouse student interest in this project

Main activity: Class discussion

Intended outcomes: 1 A clear idea of the scope of the project
2 The formation of working groups

Approximate time: ½ – 1 hour

ACTIVITIES

Teacher	Students
1 Introduce the subject of the growing importance of the English language. Suggestions: • Show a video TV programme in English or play a British or American pop song. • Ask students to guess how many people of their parents' (or grandparents') generation can speak English.	
2 Explain the idea of the project, and ask students to suggest the kinds of information they would like to find out. Here are some suggestions (only mention these if students run out of ideas): • How, where and when did people learn their English? • How many people use English in their jobs? • How many people have visited an English-speaking country? • Do people think English is important? Why?	Make suggestions.
3 Once the scope of the project has been established, discuss appropriate methods of collecting information.	Take part in discussions and make collective decisions.
4 Tell students they are going to work in groups for the rest of the project.	Form working groups.

Stage 2

Main activity: Writing/Proofreading

Lead-in activity: Discussions - Activity 1 (page 102)

Intended outcome: Survey plans

Approximate time: ½ hour

ACTIVITIES

Students (In groups formed in Stage 1)	Teacher
	Explain this stage.
1 Groups discuss and plan their information-collecting campaign. Decide: • What kind of information to collect. Examples: statistics; opinions; anecdotes; • Who to ask. Examples: general public; specific age group; students' own families and friends. • How to collect information. Examples: survey based on written questionnaire; interviews.	Monitor discussions.
2 One student notes group decisions.	Look at plans, but do not correct or comment unless asked.
3 Allocate tasks to individuals or pairs within groups. Example: each student could write one or two questions to be put to inverviewees.	

Stage 3

Main activity:	Writing
Lead-in activity:	Writing a questionnaire (page 84)
Intended outcome:	1 Survey material
	2 Final preparations for conducting survey

Approximate time:
1 hour

ACTIVITIES

Students

1 Individuals or pairs write survey questions. Decide on the most suitable form of questions for this purpose.
Keep language simple and the meaning clear.

2 Try out draft form questions on other students in the group. Use this opportunity to correct language errors, and to check that the questions give the kind of answers or information you need.

3 Re-write questions (if necessary) and combine them to make a complete questionnaire.

Teacher

Monitor writing activity and, if necessary, remind students about different question styles.
(*Note:* writing should be in English even if interviews are eventually carried out partly in students' own language.)

Monitor testing of questions and help with corrections.

Check final form of questions.

Stage 4

Main activity:	Interviewing
Intended outcome:	Collection of information

Approximate time:
1 – 3 hours

ACTIVITIES

Students

1 Before going out into the streets, practise approaching people with polite opening questions. Example: *Excuse me, we're doing a language survey. Would you mind answering a few questions?*
(If you are going to record interviews, check that the equipment is working and that you know how to use it.)

2 Carry out survey as agreed. Work in pairs. Take it in turns to ask the questions and note the answers (or operate cassette recorder). Try to interview about ten people.

3 Return to classroom.

Teacher

Set the rules for this stage: time limit; where students may go.

Monitor some interviews discreetly if possible. At least be aware of where students are.

Stage 5

Main activity:	Processing information collected	**Approximate time:**
Lead-in activity:	Expressing information in different ways (page 89)	**1 – 3 hours**
Intended outcome:	Draft form summaries of information collected	

ACTIVITIES

Students

1 Re-form working groups and talk about your interviewing experiences:
   - Discuss people's attitude to the survey.
   - Discuss how best to process the information you have collected. Think about these ways of producing concise summaries:
     ▷ Transcription of recorded interviews
     ▷ Written summary
     ▷ Chart of statistics
     ▷ Bar or pie charts
     ▷ Graphs

2 Allocate summarising tasks to pairs or individuals. Examples:
   - Pair 1 could collect and summarise all information about how, where and when people interviewed learnt their English. This might be presented in the form of a pie chart.
   - Pair 2 could summarise people's attitudes towards the growing importance of English as a world language. Here a short written summary might be appropriate.

3 Write up information.

Teacher

Monitor group discussions.

Remind students about the Lead-in Activity related to processing information. Give advice if asked for, but let students make their own decisions.

Monitor writing, but do not give direct help at this stage.

Stage 6

Main activities:	Proofreading/Rewriting	**Approximate time:**
Lead-in activity:	Proofreading (page 79)	**1 hour**
Intended outcome:	Corrected data summaries	

ACTIVITIES

Students

1 - Pairs or individuals exchange and read through each other's written summaries.
   - Check and correct any language mistakes and, if necessary, ask for clarification.

2 Discuss corrections and possible improvements.

3 Original writers rewrite summaries, paying attention to accuracy, appropriateness and presentation.

Teacher

Arbitrate in cases of disagreement over correct language forms and usage.

Remind students that clarity, accuracy and visual presentation are important at this stage.

Stage 7

Main activities:	Display/Reporting back/Class discussion	**Approximate time:**
Lead-in activity:	Giving a short talk (page 79)	**1 hour**
Intended outcome:	Class awareness of survey findings and conclusions	

ACTIVITIES

Students	**Teacher**
1 Display all results of survey in classroom. All groups examine what others have produced	Help with display organisation.
2 In turn, each group gives a verbal report of the work they have done for this project. This may involve anecdotes about street interviews, factual details from the survey, playing recorded conversations, etc.	
3 Groups question each other about their findings.	Join in the questioning.
4 Whole class discussion covering:	Take part in this final discussion.

• The findings of the survey:
  What conclusions can we draw about the state of English language learning in our country?
• The working methods:
  How interesting or successful has the project been, both in its own right and as a language learning activity?

3 YOUNG PERSON'S GUIDE TO YOUR TOWN

1 Suitability

Level .... Elementary/Intermediate
Age: .... Secondary/Young adults
Class: .... It will be an advantage if students are already familiar with the town in which they are studying
Approximate time: .... 8–12 hours

2 Project description

In this project students are going to produce a Young Person's Guide to the town in which they are studying. This guide should be aimed at young English-speaking people who may visit the town in the future. It should be a lively alternative to any official town guides, which may be rather 'stuffy' or irrelevant to the needs and interests of young people. It is important that, from the beginning, students are encouraged to look at and 'explore' the town through the eyes of these potential future visitors.

All the activities described in the stage-by-stage guide can be done in the classroom, but students may produce a more interesting guide if they are allowed to go into the town to collect information.

3 Variations

- Classes studying in Britain should write a guide for future elementary or intermediate classes of foreign students.
- The guide may be aimed at a specific group of young people. Examples:
  1 an exchange group whose visit is already arranged.
  2 a visiting sports team.
  3 students who come to do holiday jobs in or near your town.
- The guide may contain general information about life in your country. Examples: public transport/money matters/visits to the doctor and dentist, etc.
- If you live in a large town or a city, restrict the guide to the area your students know best.

4 End product

Format:
- A booklet which can be reproduced cheaply
- The booklet should be visually attractive as well as informative

Contents: Include sections on some of the following subjects:
- Places to eat and drink
- Tourist attractions
- Where to get help and advice
- Getting around (Transport)
- Where to meet other young people
- 'Value-for-money' shops
- Discos, clubs, cinemas
- History/famous inhabitants
- Banks
- Sports facilities
- Maps, short cuts

5 Summary of stages

Stage	Main activities	Outcome	Time (hours)
1	Class discussion	Idea of scope of project	½–1
2	Group discussions	Group plans	½–1
3	Research/Writing	Information in note form	1½–2
4	Writing/Proofreading	First draft of guide	1½–2
5	Discussion/Rewriting	Final texts/Agreed format	1–1½
6	Reporting/Discussion	Display	1
7	Production	The Town Guide	2–3
		Total anticipated time	8–11½ hours

6 Resources

- Existing town guides
- Maps
- Local newspapers
- Camera
- Access to a typewriter and photocopier
- Local libraries
- Tourist information offices

7 Location

- Stages 1, 2, 3, 6, 7 – the classroom.
- Stage 3 – town (in or out of school time)
- Stages 4, 5 – classroom or home.

8 Lead-in activities

9   Stage-by-stage guide

Stage 1 – Introduction

Aim: To arouse students' interest in this project
Main activity: Class discussion
Intended outcomes: 1 Clear decisions about the scope and contents of the guide
2 The formation of working groups or pairs of students

Approximate time:
½ –1 hour

ACTIVITIES

Teacher

1 Introduce the topic in a way which will arouse the interest of the class. Suggestions:
 • Get students to look at and comment on existing town guides (these may be in their own language). Discuss how they might be improved for young visitors.
 • Get students to imagine they are visiting a foreign town for the first time. What information would they like and/or do they need to know?

2 Introduce the project idea and ask students to suggest the contents of the guide. There is a list of suggestions in the Contents of the End Product section, but do not refer to these until students have had a chance to come up with ideas of their own.

3 Discuss guide format: length, size, etc.

4 Discuss working methods:
 • Where should information come from?
 • How should it be collected?
 • How can tasks be divided amongst the class?

5 Tell students they are going to work in pairs or groups for the rest of the project. Each group should choose one section of the guide.

Students

Discuss in pairs.

Class discussion.

Volunteer ideas.

Suggest content ideas.

Make suggestions.

Discuss and make decisions

Form working pairs or groups according to interests.

Stage 2

Main activity: Group discussions
Lead-in activity: Discussions - Activity 2 (page 102)
Intended outcome: Groups' plans/Written notes of decisions

Approximate time:
½ –1 hour

ACTIVITIES

Students
(In groups formed in Stage 1)

1 Groups plan the content of the section of the guide they have chosen. Discuss how the section might be sub-divided. Example:
Shop group
 • Shops that sell the kinds of things young people buy
 • Shops that are good value for money
 • Shops to be avoided at all costs

2 Make written notes of all plans and decisions.

3 Discuss how to collect information:
 • What sort of information to collect
 • Where to look for information, etc.

4 Share out the tasks to pairs or individuals in the groups. Example:
 • Sporting facilities
  Pair 1 - Indoor sports
  Pair 2 - Outdoor sports, etc.

Teacher
Explain this stage. Set time limit.
Monitor discussions, giving advice if it is asked for.

Look at notes and comment.

Monitor.

Stage 3	
Main activities: Research/Writing	**Approximate time:**
Intended outcome: Information in note form	1½ – 2 hours

ACTIVITIES

Students

(Working individually or in pairs)

1 Information collecting might involve students in some of these activities:
   - Reading local newspapers - making notes
   - Doing survey of shops, cafes, etc.*
   - Drawing maps of interesting walks, tourist routes, etc.
   - Visiting the local library*
   - Checking exchange rates at banks*
   - Finding suitable visual material
   - Surveying sports and other leisure facilities*
   - Visiting the station to collect timetables*
   * These are out-of-class tasks.

2 Before leaving the classroom, write out a questionnaire or 'grid' to fill in as you go round the town. Example: Sports group

Place	Activity	Open	Closed	Price
Sports Centre	Swimming	9.00	22.00	15FF

3 Collect information.

Teacher

Explain this stage, and give clear rules to students going into the town. Check groups' plans and get sketch maps showing students' intended routes and places to be visited.

Make it clear when students should return to the classroom.

Monitor students if at all possible.

Stage 4	
Main activities: Writing/Proofreading	**Approximate time:**
Lead-in activities: Expressing information in different ways (page 89) Proofreading (page 81)	1½ – 2 hours
Intended outcome: Draft versions of guide sections	

ACTIVITIES

Students

1 Individuals and pairs return to the classroom and discuss briefly the information they have collected.

2 Individuals and pairs now write up the information in a form suitable for the guide. Examples:
   - Short continuous prose texts
   - Tables of information, e.g. times, dates, prices, etc.
   - Use headings and sub-headings
   - Illustrate with photographs, maps, plans, sketches
   Do not write too much: only include useful or interesting information.

3 Exchange written work with another student or pair of students. Read and correct what they have written, questioning the writer about the meaning where necessary.

4 Return written work to writer(s).

Teacher

Explain this stage.
Check information collected.

Monitor this writing activity, giving help only with vocabulary.

Remind students of the idea of proofreading. Monitor this correcting stage, but intervene only in cases of disagreement.

Stage 5		Approximate time:
Main activities:	Discussion/Rewriting	**1 – 1½ hours**
Lead-in activity:	Discussions – Activity 1 (page 102)	
Intended outcome:	Final versions of guide sections	

ACTIVITIES

Students	Teacher
	Explain this stage.
1 Start with short whole class discussion to decide on the final format of the guide in the light of the information that has been collected. Agree on: length of whole guide/length and order of the sections. Groups should sit together and argue the importance of their section.	Take part in this discussion.
2 Once agreement has been reached, pairs or individuals rewrite their own material bearing in mind the proofreader's comments and the class decisions about guide format. (This may involve shortening or lengthening your first draft.) Carefully redraw maps and other illustrations.	Monitor and give help if it is asked for. Remind students that clarity and accuracy are important at this stage.
3 If a camera is available, this would be a good time to take photographs.	

Stage 6		Approximate time:
Main activities:	Reporting back/Discussion	**1 hour**
Lead-in activity:	Giving a short talk (page 79)	
Intended outcomes:	1 Whole class awareness of what has been produced 2 Classroom display	

ACTIVITIES

Students	Teacher
	Explain this stage.
1 Remain in pairs and prepare short talks, describing the work they have been doing.	
2 Display all material in the classroom.	Allow time for all students to look at each other's work.
3 Pairs or individuals give prepared talks, referring to the display where appropriate. Talks, which should last about one minute, should be given with the help of notes. (They should not simply be read.) After each talk the rest of the class comments or ask questions.	Take part in this commenting and questioning.

Stage 7	Approximate
Main activity: Production of the guide	**time:**
Intended outcome: Final copy of guide in booklet form, ready to be reproduced	**2 – 3 hours**

ACTIVITIES

Students

A small volunteer group of enthusiasts could take on the job of combining the work of all groups to produce the guide.

This is a practical task, which might best be done by artistic students who have an eye for what is visually attractive. Tasks may include:

- Cutting and sticking
- Typing handwritten texts
- Experimenting with different layouts
- Photocopying - reducing, enlarging, etc.
- Designing a front cover

(*Note:* If the finished guide is attractive enough, why not make copies to give to other students? Your local tourist information office may even be interested in taking copies!)

Teacher

Give practical help wherever possible, but do not do the work yourself. This is a student production.

4 BRITISH OR AMERICAN INFLUENCE ON YOUR WAY OF LIFE

1 Suitability

Level .... Intermediate/Advanced
Age: .... Any
Class: .... This project is intended for a class studying in their own country. If you are working in an English-speaking country, see Variations

Approximate time: .... 9–13 hours

2 Project description

The aim of this project is to study the influence of Britain or America on the way of life in your country. Students may focus their attention on a wide range of influences from eating habits to politics, and from pop music to everyday language. Clearly, the aspects of the subject chosen will depend on the students' age, interests and level of ability. Before dividing the class into groups, spend time discussing the extent of these influences, some of which may not have occurred to students before.

If it is practical in your teaching circumstances, allow students to conduct an opinion survey in your town, to investigate how the general public perceive and react to British and American influences.

3 Variations

- If students are working in Britain, they could study the American influence on the British way of life.
- If it is impractical to allow students to conduct research outside the classroom, the opinions of relatives and friends, especially of their parents' generation, could be investigated.
- More advanced classes might study the growth of British or American influences during the last ten or twenty years.

4 End product

Format:
- A written report and/or a classroom display
- The report/display could consist of written descriptions, the results of opinion surveys, photographs, realia (e.g. typical British or American products), video extracts of TV programmes

Contents: Some ideas:
- The spread of 'fast food' restaurants (e.g. McDonalds)
- British/American singers and groups in your Top 20 (record sales)
- The use of English (British or American varieties) in your everyday language
- The effects of American air bases on the areas in which they are situated
- British/American street fashions
- Media – imports of television programmes, films, etc.

5 Summary of stages

Stage	Main activities	Outcome	Time (hours)
1	Class discussion	Idea of scope of project	½–1
2	Group discussions	Plans/Allocation of tasks	1
3	Research (1)	Collection of information	1–3
4	Research (2): Survey	Collection of information	2
5	Processing of information	First draft reports	2
6	Proofreading/Rewriting	Final version reports	1–2
7	Reporting/Discussion	Project conclusions	1–2
		Total anticipated time	8½–13 hours

6 Resources

- Printed: newspapers, magazines, radio and TV programme guides
- People who are prepared to answer survey questions
- Places to visit, study and report on, e.g. restaurants, shops
- Television (at home?)
- A cassette recorder for interviews

7 Location

- Stages 1, 2, 7 – the classroom.
- Stages 3, 4 – town or home.
- Stages 5, 6 – classroom or home.

8 Lead-in activities

9   Stage-by-stage guide

Stage 1 – Introduction

Aim: To arouse students' interest in the project

Main activity: Class discussion

Intended outcomes: 1 A clear idea of the scope and contents of the investigation

2 The formation of groups or pairs of students to work on specific aspects of the subject

Approximate time:
½ –1 hour

ACTIVITIES

Teacher

Students

1 Introduce the topic in a thought-provoking way.
Suggestions:
- Show a video of TV commercials using American settings. E.g.: Coca Cola, Levi jeans.
- Do a survey of the class to find out how many students have T-shirts with slogans in English.
- Do a survey to find out how many students have eaten hamburgers during the last week.

2 • Introduce the project idea and ask students to suggest what aspects of life in their country are most influenced by Britain or America.
(*Note:* There is a list of suggestions in the Contents of the End Product section, but do not refer to these until students have had a chance to come up with ideas of their own.)
- Make a list of students' suggestions and discuss each in turn.

(Students column) Make suggestions.

(Students column) Class discussion.
Form working groups.

3 Once the scope of the project has been established, students should choose a subject which interests them and form working groups.

Stage 2

Main activity: Group discussions

Lead-in activity: Discussions - Activity 1 (page 102)

Intended outcome: Groups' plans/Written notes of decisions

Approximate time:
1 hour

ACTIVITIES

Students
(In groups formed in Stage 1)

Teacher
Explain this stage. Set time limit of one hour.

Monitor discussions.

1 Groups plan their information-collecting campaign. Decide on main headings followed by more detailed notes. Examples:
- **Media group**
  - ▷ Television: Survey of country's TV output. *How many programmes are made in Britain or USA?* Opinion survey: *What do people think about imported programmes?*
  - ▷ Cinema: Film survey. *How are British or American films different from home-produced films?*
  - ▷ The Press: *Are British/American newspapers easy to buy? Who reads them?*
- **Food group**
  Survey of 'fast food' restaurants in your town.
  What sorts of food do they sell?
  How different is this from traditional food?
  What sort of people eat in these places?

2 • Discuss how and where information could be collected.
- Share out specific tasks among individuals or pairs in the groups.

(Teacher column) Monitor. Make sure that groups' plans are practical. Give advice if asked.

Stage 3

Main activities:	Research (1): Reading/Writing notes	**Approximate time:**
Lead-in activity:	Using a dictionary (page 103)	**1 – 3 hours**
Intended outcome:	Collection of information	

ACTIVITIES

Students

1 • Pairs or individuals start collecting information, following plans worked out in Stage 2. Much of this work could be done in the students' own time - perhaps as a series of homeworks over the period of a week.
  • Students' activities will vary according to the subject they have chosen to study, but activities might include:
    ▷ Going through telephone directory, checking how many fast food restaurants there are.
    ▷ Looking through TV guides, and watching selected programmes.
    ▷ Studying this week's pop music charts and comparing them with charts of twenty, ten and five years ago.
    ▷ Doing a survey of popular newspapers and magazines, listing all English words used.

2 Make written notes of all information collected. This will be incorporated in the final report of each group, and may be of help in preparation for the next stage of the project.

Teacher

Explain this stage. Set time limit. If students are working in their own time, allow 5 – 10 minutes at the beginnings or the ends of lessons to check their progress.

Check notes to see that students are making progress.

Stage 4

Main activities:	Research (2): Conducting a public opinion survey	**Approximate time:**
Lead-in activity:	Writing a questionnaire (page 84)	**2 hours**
Intended outcome:	Collection of information	

ACTIVITIES

Students

1 • Individuals or pairs discuss exactly what information they want to get from their surveys.
  • Write survey questions, keeping the language simple and the meaning clear.
  • Discuss ways of recording information: e.g. on cassette or in writing. (*Note:* Writing should be in English, even if interviews are eventually carried out partly in the students' own language.)

2 Try out draft questions on other students in the group. Use this opportunity to correct language errors and to check that the questions produce the kind of information you need.

3 • Rewrite questions if necessary.
  • Before going out into the town, practise approaching people politely. Example:
  Excuse me, we're doing a survey to find out how many American programmes people watch on television. Would you mind answering a few questions?

4 • Carry out survey as planned. Take it in turns to ask questions and note answers. Each pair should try to interview about ten people.
  • Return to the classroom.

Teacher

Explain this stage and remind students of the different styles of questions they can use in questionnaires.

Monitor testing of questions and help with corrections.

Check final questionnaires. Check students know how to approach people.

Monitor students discreetly if possible. At least be aware of where students are.

Stage 5

		Approximate time: 2 hours
Main activities:	Processing information collected in Stages 3 and 4	
Lead-in activity:	Expressing information in different ways (page 89)	
Intended outcome:	Draft form summaries of information collected	

ACTIVITIES

Students

1 Re-form working groups and discuss how the results of your opinion survey might be summarised and presented.

Discuss how best to combine the two kinds of information collected. This may involve a simple report comprising research findings from Stage 3 (the 'facts') followed by a summary of public perceptions of and reactions to these 'facts'.

2 Individuals or pairs now summarise the information they have collected in Stages 3 and 4
- Written reports
- Statistical charts and tables
- Bar charts, pie charts, graphs

(*Note:* If interviews were recorded, transcribe answers and select interesting quotations to use in your reports.)

Teacher

Monitor this information-processing stage carefully. Students may have collected a lot of information and so may need advice about how best to organise it.

Remind students about the Lead-in Activity related to the processing of information.

Stage 6

		Approximate time: 1–2 hours
Main activities:	Proofreading/Rewriting	
Lead-in activity:	Proofreading (page 81)	
Intended outcome:	Final, corrected reports	

ACTIVITIES

Students

1
- Once written work is complete, pairs or individuals read through and check each other's information summaries.
- Check and correct any language mistakes, and ask writers for an explanation of any points that are not clear.

2 Discuss corrections and suggested improvements.

3 Original writers rewrite summaries, paying particular attention to accuracy, appropriateness and presentation.

Teacher

Help resolve any disagreements over correct language forms and usage.

Remind students that clarity and accuracy are important at this stage.

	Stage 7	
Main activities:	Reporting back/Classroom display/ Discussion	**Approximate time:**
Lead-in activity:	Giving a short talk (page 79)	**1 – 2 hours**
Intended outcome:	Project conclusions	

ACTIVITIES

Students

1 Display the results of research in the classroom, including information summaries, photographs, other visual material and realia.

2 ● Each group in turn gives a short verbal report to the class. Individuals and pairs may report their own findings, or one student may represent the whole group. Make reference, where appropriate, to the display, and play any audio or video recordings made.
   ● Groups ask questions and/or comment on each other's presentations.

3 Final class discussion.
   ● *What conclusions have you come to about the extent of the British or American influence on your country's way of life?*
   ● *Is this influence a good or a bad thing?*
   ● *Can anything be done to stop or reverse this process?*
   ● *Are there other competing influences? Which will be the dominating influence in the year 2025 or 2050?*

Teacher

Help with display organisation.

Take part in the questioning and commenting.

Take part in this final discussion.

5 PLANNING AN EDUCATIONAL VISIT TO AN ENGLISH-SPEAKING COUNTRY

1   Suitability

Level .... Intermediate/Advanced
Age: .... Secondary/Young adults
Class: .... Students should be interested in the possibility of travelling to an English-speaking country, even if this project does not lead directly to a specific visit

Approximate time: .... 6–10 hours

2   Project description

This is primarily an 'information collecting' project in which groups of students investigate and compare available educational visits. One group might study the possibility of an exchange visit with a school abroad, while another might investigate the language courses offered by commercial organisations. When all the relevant information has been collected, groups might focus on topics such as comparative costs, locations, types of visit, accommodation and other practical considerations.

To turn this project into a genuinely authentic activity, by going ahead with a real visit, would be the most fitting end product, but it is recognised that this would be impractical in many situations.

3   Variations

- The focus of the project might be a comparative study of summer courses in Britain or the USA.
- A more modest version of this theme would be 'Getting from your country to Britain (or the USA)'. Different groups could study the various possible means of transport: air, sea, rail and road.
- The meaning of 'educational visit' can be interpreted as widely as you wish. Some classes, for example, might investigate a geographical/geological visit, or a literary tour of Great Britain, etc.

4   End product

Format:
- A brochure, aimed at the parents of potential 'customers', describing the alternative visits investigated by the different groups of students
- The detailed programme of a visit, or a real visit

(*Note:* The production of an actual brochure, or the planning of a real visit will extend this project well beyond the 6–10 hours suggested.)

Contents:
- Brochure version 1 (Alternative types of visit)
  Section 1: Exchange visits
  Section 2: Language courses
  Section 3: Specialist interest visits
- Brochure version 2 (Comparisons)
  Section 1: Choice of places to visit; places to stay
  Section 2: Choice of methods of transport
  Section 3: Choice of types of visit available (summary)
  Section 4: Comparative costs – what is best value for money?
  Section 5: Opinions of people who have experienced educational visits

5   Summary of stages

Stage	Main activities	Outcome	Time (hours)
1	Class discussion	Idea of scope of project	½–1
2	Group discussion	Plans/Allocation of tasks	½–1
3	Research	Information about visits	2–3
4	Reporting back/Processing of information	First draft summaries	1–1½
5	Proofreading/Rewriting	Final version summaries	1–1½
6	Reporting back/Display/Class discussion	Sharing of information/Conclusions/Decisions	1–2
		Total anticipated time	6–10 hours

6   Resources

- Publicity material produced by commercial holiday course companies.
- Prospectuses of language schools in Britain or USA.
- Maps and tourist information about selected towns and regions.
- Travel information: travel agency brochures, timetables, etc.

7   Location

- Stages 1, 2, 5, 6 – the classroom.
- Stage 3 – the classroom, your school, another school, or home
- Stage 4 – classroom or home.

8   Lead-in activities

9   Stage-by-stage guide

Stage 1 – Introduction

Aim:	To arouse students' interest in the project	**Approximate time:**
Main activity:	Class discussion	½ – 1 hour
Intended outcomes:	1 A clear idea of the scope of the project	
	2 The formation of working groups	

ACTIVITIES

Teacher

1 Introduce the topic of educational visits.
 Suggestions:
 ● Class survey: *How many times have students been abroad/to an English-speaking country? Have any of them been on an educational visit? Were their visits really educational?*
 ● Show class some brochures from educational/summer language course companies. Discuss the pros and cons of these kinds of courses.

2 Tell students they are going to plan an educational visit for themselves. Ask for suggestions about:
 ● the main purpose of a visit
 ● places they would like to visit
 ● the length of the visit/possible dates
 Checklist of ideas:
 Purposes: cultural experience/language improvement
 Places: GB/USA/Australia, etc.
 Time: 1-3 weeks/Spring or Summer

3 Once the scope of the project has been established, suggest that students form groups to work on specific aspects of the theme. Examples:
 ● travel ● accommodation ● costs
 ● educational programme ● leisure activities ● language courses, etc.

Students

Discuss as whole class or in small groups.

Volunteer ideas and opinions.

Discuss as whole class or in groups and make suggestions.

Decide on division of the subject, and form working groups.

Stage 2

Main activity:	Group discussion	**Approximate time:**
Lead-in activity:	Discussions - Activity 2 (page 102)	½ – 1 hour
Intended outcome:	Groups' plan/written notes/the allocation of tasks	

ACTIVITIES

Students
(In groups formed in Stage 1)

1 Groups plan information-collecting tasks and make a written note of their decisions. Example:
 Travel group notes:
 ● Choice of methods of travelling
 ● Investigate costs and convenience
 ● Do survey of travel preferences of other students
 ● Summarise pros and cons of each method

2 Discuss research methods. Examples:
 ● Where to find travel information
 ● How to conduct survey

3 Share out specific tasks among pairs or individuals on the basis of interest and ability.

Teacher
Explain this stage and set a time limit.

Monitor discussions and get students to explain, from notes they have made, how they are going to proceed.

Give advice about working methods, and check that plans are practical.

Stage 3

Main activity:	Research	
Lead-in activities:	Writing a questionnaire (page 84) Conducting an interview (page 87) Making notes (page 92) Writing letters (page 97)	**Approximate time:** **2 – 3 hours**
Intended outcome:	Detailed information about various aspects of the planned visit	

ACTIVITIES

Students

(*Note:* During this stage individuals or groups may find it useful to consult each other.)

Pairs or individuals start collecting information about their chosen aspect of the subject. Working methods will vary from group to group, but tasks may include:
* visiting a travel agency
* working out costs (checking the Press for exchange rates, etc.)
* writing letters to language schools asking for information about their courses
* contacting tourist offices in the country to be visited
* interviewing other students who have already been on visits
* writing a questionnaire and carrying out an opinion survey

Many of these tasks may be done outside class time.

Teacher

Explain the stage, set a time limit and make the rules clear. (E.g.: can students leave the school/use the telephone?)

Tell students what resources and equipment are available for them to use, e.g. cassette recorders, libraries, etc.

Monitor as many of these activities as possible.

Stage 4

Main activities:	Reporting back/Processing information collected in Stage 3	
Lead-in activity:	Expressing information in different ways (page 89)	**Approximate time:** **1 – 1½ hours**
Intended outcome:	Draft form summaries of information collected	

ACTIVITIES

Students

1 Individuals or pairs report back to their groups. Groups discuss information and, if necessary, revise previous decisions and plans. Decide on the form of presentation that best suits the types of information collected. Examples:
   * Travel Group: table of comparative costs/maps showing various travel options
   * Information on towns and regions: brief written descriptions/maps/ photographs/recordings or transcripts of comments made by students who have already been on visits, etc.

2 In the light of group discussions and using notes made during Stage 3, write first draft summaries of information collected.
   At this stage, attention should be focused on expressing information clearly. Avoid long complicated written reports by using graphs, tables of figures, maps, charts, etc.

Teacher

Explain this stage.

Monitor discussions and ask questions for information.

Monitor this writing stage, making a note of difficulties, but giving help only where absolutely necessary.

Stage 5

Main activities:	Proofreading/Rewriting	**Approximate time:** 1 – 1½ hours
Lead-in activity:	Proofreading (page 81)	
Intended outcome:	Final, corrected, versions of information summaries	

ACTIVITIES

Students

1 Students proofread each other's first draft summaries, correcting language mistakes and asking writers questions to clarify points of information.

2 Before draft summaries are rewritten, groups discuss how the information may be presented in an interesting and attractive way in the brochure.

3 Individuals rewrite their information summaries, incorporating corrections and presentation suggestions. At this stage, students should be aiming to present information in a clear, accurate and attractive way.

Teacher

Arbitrate in cases of disagreement over correct forms of language.

Monitor discussions and give advice if asked.

Remind students that clarity and accuracy are important, but do not intervene once students have started writing.

Stage 6

Main activities:	Reporting back/Putting on a display/ Discussion	**Approximate time:** 1 – 2 hours
Lead-in activity:	Giving a short talk (page 79)	
Intended outcome:	Class awareness of the work of all groups/ Decision about how to make use of information collected	

ACTIVITIES

Students

1 Display the final versions of brochure sections around the classroom.

2 Each group in turn gives a short verbal report to the rest of the class, referring where appropriate to their display. Individuals or pairs may report their own findings, or one student may represent the group.
Groups ask questions or comment on each other's presentations.

3 Class discussion: *What kind of educational visit would students choose in the light of all the information that has been collected and presented?*

4 If the class wishes, discuss and decide how to use the information collected. Possible uses:
● Produce a brochure containing all information.
● Produce an 'ideal programme' for an educational visit.
● Plan a real visit.

Teacher

Take part in this questioning and commenting session.

Take part in this discussion.

Ask students whether they would like to take this project a stage further.

6 STARTING A SELF-ACCESS READING RESOURCES BANK

1 Suitability

Level .... Upper Intermediate/Advanced
Age: .... Secondary/adults
Class: .... Most suitable for well-motivated students who are accustomed to working with authentic reading texts

Approximate time: .... 4–6 hours

2 Project description

The aim of this project is the production of a self-access reading resource bank. Students should select interesting texts and write accompanying exercises suitable for use by students of English at elementary or intermediate level. Although in the first instance it is designed to last 3½–6 hours, it may be regarded as a continuing project which can be extended indefinitely to produce an expanding resource collection.

The project activities will provide useful language practice for the students involved, while the end product should benefit the school as a whole. The initial class discussion (Stage 1) is of great importance in motivating students; they should not be given the impression that they are being asked to do the teacher's job for him/her.

3 Variations

- As an alternative (or in addition) to reading resources, students may produce listening materials.
- This could be a joint project involving advanced students and English teachers.
- Intermediate students might be asked to work only on the selection of texts and the testing of materials. Teachers might prefer to write the accompanying exercises themselves.

4 End product

- A collection of authentic reading texts with accompanying exercises and separate answer sheet.
- Texts should be classified by theme and/or level of difficulty, and be made available to other students.

5 Summary of stages

Stage	Main activities	Outcome	Time (hours)
1	Class discussion	Idea of scope of project	½–1
2	Planning/Text selection	Collection of suitable texts	1–2
3	Reading/Writing	First draft of exercises	1–1½
4	Testing/Rewriting	Final draft of exercises	1–1½
		Total anticipated time	3½–6 hours

6 Resources

Essential:
- A supply of English language publications which may be cut up and used as individual texts, e.g. newspapers, magazines, books, brochures, leaflets, advertisements, etc.
(If necessary, organise the collection of suitable publications before formally starting the project. Possible sources are suggested in Chapter 2 Resources (page 11).
- English-language books which use authentic texts. These should be available for reference when students reach the exercise-writing stage.

Additional:
- Access to typewriters would enable students to produce more professional looking exercises to accompany texts.

7 Location

- Stages 1, 2, 4 – the classroom.
- Stage 3 – the classroom or home

8 Lead-in activities

- Using a dictionary (Stage 3) .... page 103
- Proofreading (Stage 4) .... page 81

9   **Stage-by-stage guide**

Stage 1 – Introduction

Aim: To interest students in this project

Main activity: Class discussion

Intended outcomes: 1 A clear idea of the scope of the project
2 The formation of working groups

Approximate time:
$^{1}/_{2}$ – 1 hour

ACTIVITIES

Teacher

1 Introduce the topic. Suggestions:
   - Do a class survey: *What are students' main interests outside school?/How far are their interests catered for by the kinds of texts they have to read in their English textbooks? What subjects are students tired of reading about in their English books?*
   - Give students a selection of English textbooks used in your school. Ask them to look quickly through these books and make a list of the authentic texts which they would be interested in reading. From these lists make a list of the ten most popular topics.
2 Explain the aim of this project: to produce a collection of self-access reading resources for other students in the school. Discuss:
   - Sources of original texts
   - Criteria for selection of texts: subject matter; level of difficulty; visual appeal; length, etc.
   - Appropriate exercise types
3 Suggest that students form groups to work on specific themes in which they have expressed an interest.

Students

Discuss as a whole class or in small groups.

Students work in small discussion groups.

Make suggestions and volunteer ideas and opinions.

Form working groups according to interests.

Stage 2

Main activities: Planning/Text selection

Intended outcome: Collection of suitable authentic texts and brief notes about their suitability and use

Approximate time:
1 – 2 hours

ACTIVITIES

Students
(In groups formed in Stage 1)

1 Groups discuss briefly the kinds of texts they are looking for, keeping in mind the criteria established in Stage 1.
2 Look through available materials and make initial selections. This is best done in pairs, so that students discuss the reasons for their choices.
3 Cut out or copy selected texts.
4 Make brief notes about each text:
   - Why did it attract you?
   - Who is it suitable for?
   - How could it be used?
Students might record these ideas on a form, like this:

Teacher

Explain this stage and provide resources.

Monitor discussions, giving advice where necessary.

Do not interrupt this activity. It is important that students are allowed a free choice of texts.

Monitor note-making activity, but do not intervene.

Text	Subject	Source	Level E/I*	Exercise ideas
1				
2				

*E = Elementary,
I = Intermediate

Stage 3

Main activities:	Reading/Writing	**Approximate time:**
Lead-in activity:	Using a dictionary (page 103)	**1 – 1½ hours**
Intended outcome:	First draft of exercises to accompany texts	

ACTIVITIES

Students

1 Groups allocate selected texts to individuals. Texts may be shortened if necessary but they should not be simplified.

2 Decide first which level texts are suitable for, i.e. elementary or intermediate.

3 Write at least three exercises to accompany each text. Use exercise types that you have seen in textbooks you have examined. Examples:
   - Comprehension: open-ended questions; multiple-choice questions; true/false statements
   - Vocabulary: match words and meanings; check difference in meaning between pairs of words; find verbs in the text related to these nouns: . . .
   - Summary writing
   - Inferring meaning: reading between the lines
   - Re-ordering a jumbled text.

4 Write exercises neatly so that they can be tested by another student in the group.

Teacher

Give guidance about suitability of texts for particular levels.

Monitor this activity carefully so that students do not waste time writing inappropriate exercises.

Point out various exercise types in textbooks.

Stage 4

Main activities:	Testing/Rewriting	**Approximate time:**
Lead-in activity:	Proofreading (page 81)	**1 – 1½ hours**
Intended outcome:	Final versions of exercises	

ACTIVITIES

Students

1 Exchange texts and exercises with another student in the same group.

2 Work through exercises twice:
   - to check and correct the language
   - to check that exercises work

   Ask the student who wrote the exercises for clarification of any exercises or instructions you do not understand.
   (*Note:* since this is intended as self-access material for lower level students, it is particularly important that the instructions which introduce each exercise are clearly worded.)

3 In pairs, discuss changes or improvements to the texts, exercises and instructions.

4 Write final correct versions of exercises. Write an answer sheet to accompany each set of exercises.

5 Arrange for elementary or intermediate students to try the material.

Teacher

As students work through exercises, go round the class checking what has been written.

Give help and advice where necessary.

Arbitrate in cases of disagreement.

Check final versions carefully. If this material is going to be used by other students, the language must be accurate.

PROJECT FRAMEWORKS

1 ORGANISING A BRITISH EVENING

Suitability

Level: Elementary/Intermediate
Age: Young adult students
Class: Students who already know each other well

Project description

Basic: This 'performance' project is suitable for students who have already experienced independent project work procedures. Students form interest groups and work on an activity which will form part of the programme. Because of the nature of the end product, this project is best done over an extended period of time, for example a half or a full school term. The final success of the performance will depend on student interest and motivation, so do not force students to involve themselves in activities which they do not feel are right for them.

Students should be responsible for the performance and organisational aspects of the event.

Variations/Extensions:
- The performance could be accompanied by a classroom display
- Rather than an evening, extend the project to take a whole day
- Instead of a British evening, make it an American or an Australian evening
- Involve students from a number of classes of different levels

End product

Format: A performance or show to which other students or perhaps members of the public might be invited.
Contents: A programme of English language activities. Examples: songs; playlets; films and videos; food and drink; games

Main activities

- Speaking: discussions, short talks
- Reading: recipes, plays
- Writing: notes, letters, programme for the evening
- The performance in English of programme items chosen

Resources

- A performance and display area (e.g. classroom/hall)
- Records and/or musical instruments ● Video playback or film projector ● Recipe books ● British games ● Travel books, brochures
- Visiting speakers

Lead-in activities

- Discussions: .... page 102
- Writing Letters .... page 97

Stage-by-stage development suggestions

1 Introduce the idea of a British evening and ask for suggestions about what such an event might consist of. Allow students to come up with ideas which interest them, but bear these possibilities in mind:
   - Only English should be spoken on the evening
   - Prepare British food and drinks
   - Play British games or games in English
   - Show English-language video or film
   - Listen to and/or sing British or American songs - traditional or modern
   - Organise a classroom display. Examples:
     ▷ photos of students' previous visits to an English-speaking country
     ▷ students' artistic impressions of life in Britain
     ▷ some of the more interesting work done in previous term's English lessons
   - Short talks about aspects of life in Britain, either by students or by English-speaking people living in your country.

2 Make preliminary organisational decisions:
   - Fix a date, time and venue
   - Clear with school authorities
   - Decide who to invite: other students, parents and friends, members of the public?
   - Discuss finances - how will costs be met? Ideas: charge for tickets; school petty cash; parental contributions; commercial sponsorship; students themselves.

3 Discuss working methods - how should tasks be shared out?
   - Should students work individually, in pairs or in groups?
   - Make decisions about who is going to do what.

4 Divide class according to the decisions made in 3. Examples of responsibilities:
   - **Group 1: British/American Music**
     ▷ Find a variety of recorded music to play - pop, folk, classical, brass band
     ▷ Learn song(s) to perform on the evening
     ▷ Find out and prepare short talks about favourite groups
   - **Group 2: British/American food and drink**
     ▷ Find British/American recipes and practise preparing food, e.g. scones, steak and kidney pie, hamburgers, pancakes, pumpkin pie, jelly, cups of tea, etc. (Alternatively find source of authentic British or American food in local shops.)
     ▷ Make a visual display of aspects of British/American cookery

5 Groups come together to share ideas and decide on the final programme for the evening. This might include:
   - A dress rehearsal of student performances
   - Discussions about the order of activities
   - Displaying all materials produced
   - The allocation of organisational responsibilities.

6 Individuals, pairs or groups could be made responsible for some of the following tasks:
   - Performance areas, seating arrangements, changing-rooms, etc.
   - Publicity: the production of advertisements, posters, letters of invitation
   - Mechanical equipment: lighting, stereo, video
   - Finances.

2 THE STUDY OF A BRITISH REGION

Suitability

Level: Intermediate/Advanced
Age: All ages
Class: Students who have an interest in finding out more about Britain

Project description

Basic: This 'information' project is suitable for more academically inclined students who are prepared to research and study a region of Britain in some depth.

The choice of a specific region should take account of the likely availability of resources but, if possible, get students to choose an area which is similar in some way to the region of the country that they live in. Areas can be similar in a number of ways: geographical, economic, problems, distance from the capital, make-up of the population, history, etc.

Because the relevant information will probably have to be collected from a variety of sources, this project might best be done on a regular two-hour-a-week basis over an extended period of time, rather than as an intensive study.

Contact with people living in the chosen region would give this rather bookish project human interest and encourage students to become more personally involved than they might otherwise be.

Variations/ Extensions:
- Instead of an area of Britain, students could choose to study a region of another English-speaking country.
- Students may choose a town rather than a region.
- The project could be linked with a past or future visit to Britain by students.
- The region could be one which students have already studied in another context, e.g. in geography, history or economics lessons.
- The whole class could work on different aspects of one region, or groups could work on several aspects of different regions.
- More advanced students could develop the comparative aspect of the project, by comparing the chosen region with a region of their country.

End product

Format: Scrapbook and/or classroom display.
Contents: A collection of written pieces, maps, photographs and personal impressions

Main activities

- Speaking: discussions, short talks
- Reading: books about Britain, magazines, tourist brochures
- Writing: letters, making notes, reports, editing
- Illustrating: drawing maps, producing charts and diagrams

Resources

(*Note:* Although it is important that students themselves should research much of the information they require for this study, the teacher should try to make some basic reference material available to students throughout the project – see also Appendix, page 108).

- Access to a library or resource centre
- Videos, films, TV and radio programmes
- Magazines, newspapers, books, etc.
- Tourist information offices in your country and in Britain
- British/American embassies or consulates
- A town-twinning organisation or an exchange school
- Personal contacts of teachers or students

Lead-in activities

Stage-by-stage development suggestions

1
- Introduce this project with a film or video about Britain or with a short quiz about regions of Britain.
- Explain the idea of the project and ask students to suggest regions of Britain they would like to know more about. Write up a list of the places mentioned and find out how much students already know about them.
- Allow students to decide for themselves which region(s) they wish to study, but remind them that up-to-date information about some regions might be difficult to find.
- Discuss a suitable end product. Examples: scrapbook, classroom display, individual or group presentations, magazine.

2 Discuss working methods - how should tasks be shared out? Should students work individually, in pairs, or in groups?

Find out which aspects of the chosen region individuals would like to study, and let students group themselves accordingly. Examples:
- The physical characteristics (geography) of the region. (A group of four students.)
- Historically significant events associated with the region. (A group of three students.)
- The people of the region: their character, occupations, living standards. (A pair of students who have personal contacts in the chosen region.)
- Attractions of the region: places of tourist interest, etc. (An individual student who has visited the region.)

3 Groups plan how they are going to work. This may involve:
   ● Allocating tasks to individuals or pairs within groups
   ● Tracking down sources of information
   ● Planning visits to libraries, writing letters requesting information, writing to personal contacts

4 Plenty of time should be allowed for this stage. Researching, reading, making notes, etc. could be done in students' own time, while class time could be reserved for reporting back and group discussion activities.

5 Individual students produce the first draft of the contents of the agreed end product. These might include:
   ● Written descriptions
   ● Photographs, drawings and other illustrations
   ● Maps, charts, diagrams, tables of figures, etc.

6 Students proofread each other's work, discuss corrections and improvements and then produce final versions.

7 Classroom display of all work produced by individuals, pairs or groups. Groups report back to the whole class by giving short presentation talks about their part of the project.

8 Produce scrapbook or magazine. This might involve:
   ● A class discussion about appropriate format, length and appearance
   ● The re-editing of work produced by the groups.
   (*Note:* These final tasks may best be done by a small group of enthusiastic (and artistically inclined?) students in their own time.)

3 NEWS ABOUT YOUR COUNTRY

Suitability

Level: All levels
Age: All ages
Class: No special requirements

Project description

Basic: This idea is a variation of what is perhaps the most popular type of project work. Because it can be adapted to suit any age or level of students, it is an ideal first project.

Students should produce a collection of news stories about their own country or region which will be of interest or relevance to young people in other countries. Students may produce a traditional style publication, or design their own ideal newspaper, concentrating on the kind of stories and features which they feel are missing from existing publications. This project offers plenty of scope to students with artistic talents: in addition to writing, there will be opportunities for individuals to work on design and layout, photography and illustration.

Encourage students to concentrate on the quality of what they produce rather than mere quantity. If this first issue is a success, it may be worth producing the newspaper every term.

Variations/ Extensions:
- Instead of a newspaper, students might prefer to produce a magazine consisting of general interest features rather than current news stories.
- The newspaper could focus on school or town news.
- The newspaper could contain current news about Britain.
- Use the newspaper as part of an exchange of materials with an equivalent school abroad.
- Students could work in groups on a single aspect of a class newspaper, or different groups might prefer to produce their own newspapers.
- Combine contributions from a number of classes of different levels in a larger publication.
- Classes studying in Britain could produce a newspaper containing information or news of interest to other foreign students.
- Students might produce a radio or TV (video) news programme.

End product

Format: The first issue of a student newspaper.
Contents: To be decided by the group – depending on their interests and knowledge. (See Project description.)

Main activities

- Speaking/Listening: discussions, listening to radio news reports
- Reading: authentic newspapers, proofreading
- Writing: making notes, writing articles and headlines
- Other: illustration, design and layout

Resources

- Examples of existing English-language publications for young people, including English-language magazines published in your country and teenage magazines from Britain.
- British or American adult newspapers, both serious and popular. (Although the language level in these may be far too difficult for your students, they are useful as a source of ideas for contents, layout, headline writing, etc.)
- Local and national newspapers in your students' own language.
- Radio and TV news programmes.
- A minimum of material and equipment is needed for the newspaper project, but more ambitious classes who decide to produce a radio or TV programme will need audio and video recording equipment.

Lead-in activities

- Discussions .... page 102
- Using a dictionary .... page 103
- Making notes .... page 92
- Proofreading .... page 81
- Writing headlines .... page 100
- Expressing information in different ways .... page 89

Stage-by-stage development suggestions

1.
   - Introduce the topic by taking into the class a selection of newspapers and magazines. (If you cannot get hold of enough copies, take in a single newspaper and give a page to each pair of students.)
     - In pairs, students look at one of these publications and make brief notes about contents and appearance.
     - Get each pair of students to describe the publication they have looked at to the rest of the class.
     - Start a general discussion with the question: *If you were responsible for producing a newspaper, what would it be like?*

2. Introduce the idea of a student newspaper project. Get the class to suggest ways in which they could produce a publication of their own. Ask students to make suggestions and decisions about:
   - Format, length, appearance.
   - Balance and focus of contents - how many sections will the newspaper consist of? Possible sections might include: current news, sport, personalities, music, humour, fiction, entertainment, reviews (records, films, TV, computer games, books, etc.), fashion.
   - Working methods - would students prefer to produce their own newspaper in small groups, or contribute to a class newspaper?
   - Students divide themselves into working groups and plan their newspaper or section. This might include the allocation of tasks to pairs of students or individuals.

3 Individuals 'collect' news items from the sources discussed and write first drafts of stories and articles to be included. (These could be out-of-class activities.)

4 ● Working groups re-form and students proofread each other's writing.
  ● After short discussions about corrections and improvements, students rewrite their stories.

5 Hold an editorial meeting: the discussion could involve groups or the whole class.
  ● Decide on priorities, lead story on front page, order of sections or articles, headlines, etc.

● Consider layout, design and artwork, picture captions, etc.

6 Produce Class Newspaper Volume 1 Number 1. This might best be done by a small group of volunteer students in their own time.

   If the newspaper is interesting enough, photocopies could be made available to all students in the class and could even be distributed further afield.

4 THE ATTITUDES TO YOUR COUNTRY OF FOREIGN VISITORS

Suitability

Level: Intermediate/Advanced
Age: Secondary/Young adult
Class: Students who are mature or reliable enough to work independently, outside the classroom, without constant teacher supervision
(*Note:* A 'ready supply' of foreigners in your country (and student access to them) are essential to this project.)

Project description

Basic: This 'survey' project requires thorough preparation by the class. Because the research stage requires students to do street interviews, the teacher should be confident that students will use their time profitably and be polite to people they meet. The information, if successfully collected, should provide the basis for written work and fascinating class discussions. There are four major stages to this project: planning and preparation, street interviews, information processing, and reporting back.

Variations/ Extensions:
- The survey could focus on the attitudes of *one* group of foreigners, e.g. permanent residents, tourists, people of one age group, or people of a specific nationality.
- Students could decide to find out foreigners' attitudes to a specific issue, e.g. the future of the European Community, the problem of environmental pollution, the treatment of animals, etc.
- The focus of attention could be on facts rather than opinions, e.g. people's nationality, age, occupation, favourite sports, reasons for being abroad, etc.
- If students are studying in Britain, they might choose to interview British people about their attitudes to foreigners, or foreigners about their attitude to Britain.
- If street interviews are impractical in your situation, the survey could be based on written questionnaires.

End product

Format: Written reports, visual displays, or verbal presentations.
Contents: Results of public opinion surveys into what foreign visitors think about your town, country or people. This could be accompanied by photographs or cartoons illustrating those aspects of your country mentioned by foreigners interviewed.

Main activities

- Speaking/Listening: discussion, interviewing, presenting survey findings
- Writing: writing questionnaires, summarising survey results, writing short reports
- Other: Cartoon illustrations

Resources

- 'Human resources' are essential. In addition to those already mentioned above: foreign students on language courses, British teachers working in schools, immigrant communities.
- Places to visit: hotels, campsites, parks, beaches, cafes, tourist offices, airports, stations, universities, schools.
- English-language newspapers and magazines, especially those published in your country; TV and radio programmes (e.g. BBC World Service)
- Useful equipment might include: cassette recorders to record interviews and cameras to photograph selected foreigners and aspects of life mentioned in interviews.

Lead-in activities

Stage-by-stage development suggestions

1
- Introduce this project with a discussion about national stereotypes.
- Alternatively, if available, show a film or video illustrating a foreigner's view of life in your country.
- End with the question: *What image do foreigners have of the students' country?*

2 Discuss the project idea with the class. Decide on the focus of the survey:
- What kinds of information would be most interesting?
- What kinds of people could be asked? Are there enough foreigners in your community to make this survey possible? Do they have to be native speakers of English, or is English international enough to be used as a lingua franca by many different nationalities?

3 Discuss working methods:
- How should information be collected? E.g. street interviews, telephone calls, written questionnaire?
- How can the project topic be sub-divided?
- Students divide themselves into working groups, each taking a different aspect of the topic. Examples:
Group 1: British people/**Group 2:** Americans, etc.
or
Group 1: Tourists/**Group 2:** Business people, etc.

4 Plan and carry out the survey:
- In groups, students plan the survey, writing questionnaires, etc.
- Pairs within groups may proofread and correct each other's writing.
- Plan interview strategy: discuss where to find foreigners, how to approach people, how to ask questions and record answers, e.g. in writing or on cassette?

5 Processing survey results:
- In groups, students read and discuss survey findings.
- Write up results in an appropriate form. Examples: tables of statistics, short written reports highlighting key findings, diagrams, charts.
- Artistic students could illustrate reports with cartoons and photographs.

6 Groups present their findings to the rest of the class by means of displays, short talks, etc.

7 Extension (optional):
- Whole class discussion: How might the information from different groups be combined into a class report: *Foreigners in our Town*?
- Groups combine information. This may involve discussion and negotiation within and between groups, the rearrangement of all material from different groups and the production of a booklet.

5 THE ARTS IN BRITAIN

Suitability

Level: Upper intermediate/Advanced

Age: Upper secondary/Adults

Class: Students need no specific qualities other than a general interest in cultural matters

Project description

Basic: In this project students work in groups on an aspect of British culture which interests them. Although it is expected that groups will want to work on different topics, there should be opportunities both during and at the end of the project for students to report what they have been doing.

The words 'arts' and 'culture' may be interpreted as widely as you wish: from Shakespeare to the latest street fashions, and from 18th Century architecture to Heavy Metal Rock music. Although students should be made aware that the success of their topic may depend partly on the availability of resources, it is very important that they should be allowed to pursue a subject in which they are genuinely interested.

This project is probably best done over an extended period of time, possibly 1 – 2 hours a week for ten weeks. This will allow time for students to collect and exploit a variety of resources. It is quite possible for students to do this project in the classroom and for homework. However, they may benefit from being able to work ouside the classroom on certain occasions, for example to visit libraries, museums, etc.

Variations/ Extensions:
- Students may choose to study a cultural aspect of any English-speaking country, e.g. the life and work of Andy Warhol; the Australian cinema in the 1980s.
- Groups may choose to study different aspects of the same topic.
  Example: Folklore
  Group 1: Traditional songs
  Group 2: Contemporary songs
  Group 3: Traditional instruments
  Group 4: Traditional dances

End product

One or more of the following:
- Written reports, compositions, scrapbooks
- Presentation talks by individuals or groups
- Audio/Visual presentations with commentaries
- Individual or group performances

Main activities

- Speaking/Listening: discussions, play readings, presenting verbal reports
- Reading: books, newspaper or magazine articles, film or record reviews
- Writing: making notes, writing reports
- Other: Making a visual display, performing a play, collecting and playing recorded music

Resources

Places:
- School, university and public libraries and resource centres.
- Local cinemas, theatres, museums, art galleries, concert halls, etc.

Materials:
- Books, magazines, videos, cassettes, records, TV and radio programmes

Lead-in activities

- Discussions .... page 102
- Using a dictionary .... page 103
- Making notes .... page 92

Introduction ideas

- Show video of well-known British 'art' film. Examples: *A Passage to India*, *1984*, *Tess*, *Sons and Lovers*, etc.
- Give a quiz about British or American cultural matters.
- Ask students to suggest the names of British or American artists, painters, poets, writers, singers, composers, etc. Find out how much is known about them.

Initial decisions

- Choice of arts topics.
- Formation of working groups:
  – will groups work on related topics? Example: Cinema
  Group A: British post-war cinema
  Group B: American westerns
  Group C: The films of Sir Laurence Olivier
  Group D: Silent comedy films, etc.
  or
  – will groups work on unrelated topics. Example:
  Group A: British cinema
  Group B: 1980s street fashions
  Group C: The story of the Beatles
  Group D: The art of David Hockney, etc.
- Form of end product(s).

Arts ideas

Music	Visual arts	Performance arts	Literature
▷ Classical	▷ Painting	▷ Drama/Plays	▷ Novels
▷ Popular	▷ Sculpture	▷ Dance	▷ Poetry
▷ Folk	▷ Photography	▷ Opera	▷ Drama
▷ Jazz	▷ Cinema		
▷ Musicals	▷ Architecture		
▷ Brass bands	▷ Design		
	▷ Fashion		

Final presentation ideas

- The production of scrapbooks or a classroom display of all groups' work
- Written reports, summarised in short presentation talks
- Group or individual performances

6 BRITISH OR AMERICAN COMPANIES IN YOUR COUNTRY

Suitability

Level: All levels (Elementary, Intermediate and Advanced options are suggested)

Age: Secondary/Adults

Class: The Intermediate and Advanced options would be suitable for a class of Business English students

Project description

The idea of these frameworks is to focus student attention on the influence and image of British or American companies operating in your country. At elementary level, this could be a survey of relevant products available in your local shops. At intermediate and advanced levels, students might be expected to study in more detail the position of foreign companies in relation to national companies with which they compete.

End product

- Written, audio-visual or verbal reports summarising survey findings
- Classroom display including reports, photographs, actual products, charts, graphs, maps and diagrams

Main activities

- Writing: descriptions, letters, reports, questionnaires
- Reading: newspapers, reports, advertisements
- Speaking/Listening: discussions, interviews, reporting back, meetings, telephone conversations

Resources

- Local shops and businesses
- Advertisements
- Financial and business press
- Company publicity
- Samples or photographs of products

Lead-in activities

- Writing letters: requesting information/to invite a speaker page 97
- Conducting an interview .... page 87
- Writing a questionnaire .... page 84
- Making notes .... page 92
- Expressing information in different ways .... page 89

Collecting information

- Write to or phone companies:
  - ▷ to arrange visit
  - ▷ to arrange meeting
  - ▷ to invite representative to speak at school
- Contact company headquarters in Britain/America.
- Contact embassies.
- Do interviews with:
  - ▷ employees
  - ▷ British/American managers
- Personal contacts:
  - ▷ Students themselves
  - ▷ Families and friends
- Conduct consumer surveys.

Stage-by-stage development suggestions

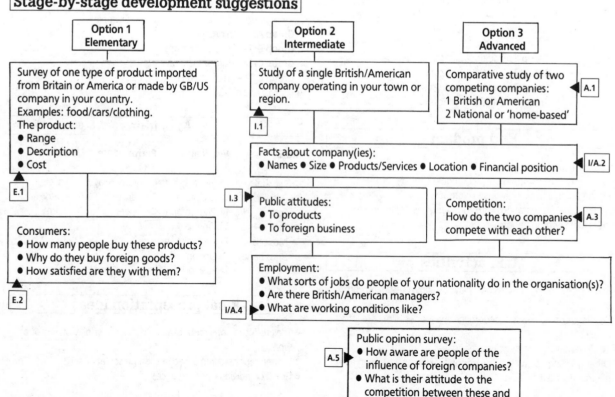

Option 1 — Elementary

Survey of one type of product imported from Britain or America or made by GB/US company in your country.
Examples: food/cars/clothing.
The product:
- Range
- Description
- Cost

E.1

Consumers:
- How many people buy these products?
- Why do they buy foreign goods?
- How satisfied are they with them?

E.2

Option 2 — Intermediate

Study of a single British/American company operating in your town or region.

I.1

Facts about company(ies):
- Names • Size • Products/Services • Location • Financial position

I/A.2

I.3

Public attitudes:
- To products
- To foreign business

Employment:
- What sorts of jobs do people of your nationality do in the organisation(s)?
- Are there British/American managers?
- What are working conditions like?

I/A.4

Option 3 — Advanced

Comparative study of two competing companies:
1 British or American
2 National or 'home-based'

A.1

Competition:
How do the two companies compete with each other?

A.3

Public opinion survey:
- How aware are people of the influence of foreign companies?
- What is their attitude to the competition between these and national companies?

A.5

7 STARTING AN ENGLISH CLUB

Suitability

Level: All levels
Age: Secondary/Adults
Class: Students should be prepared to spend time outside official school hours

Project description

It would be best to start this long-term project at, or soon after, the beginning of a school year, or at a time when you can be fairly sure that your group of students will remain together for a reasonably long period. This framework suggests ways in which students themselves can be involved in all aspects of running an English club, including the initial decisions about a suitable programme of events, the arranging of meeting places and out-of-school visits, and the writing of publicity material. Even if students prefer to use their own language in discussions, you should insist that all written work (e.g. publicity and letters) and performances (e.g. plays and songs) are in English.

End product

● The first meeting of the English Club.

Main activities

● Conducting a survey:
  ▷ What sort of club do students want?
  ▷ What talents or skills do students have?
  ▷ How much time can students devote to the club?
● Discussions: planning meetings
● Writing: letters to invite speakers/request information
           programme of meetings: notes on performers and their material
● Other: making practical arrangements and putting on performances.

Initial decisions

● Who is the club for?
  any students/one class/one level/one age group
● What are the purposes of the club?
  social/entertainment/education

● When and how often will it meet?
  after school/at weekends/weekly/monthly/irregularly
● Where will it meet?
  at school – classroom/common room
  outside school

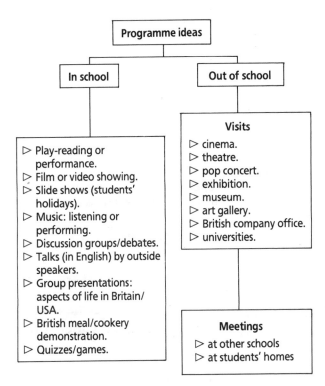

Resources

● Books, newspapers, magazines, videos, photographs
● People with specialist knowledge who might speak at a club meeting
● Radio and TV programmes

Lead-in activities

8 ENGLISH SPOKEN HERE

Suitability

Level: All levels (Elementary, Intermediate and Advanced options are suggested)

Age: All ages

Class: Students will need access to a wide range of reference materials

Project description

This broad title gives students the opportunity to work on aspects of life in any country where English is spoken.

This is an 'information' type project, which will involve students in researching information, reading and writing.

Elementary classes could study an aspect of life in a single country, for example, *The Geography of Canada*.

Intermediate and advanced students might prefer a more challenging task, for example: comparing life in two or more countries, researching the historical reasons for the fact that English is spoken outside Britain, or comparing several varieties of English.

End product

A scrapbook, written report, classroom display.
(*Note:* The precise format of the end product will depend upon the particular topics chosen and on the level of the class.)

Main activities

- Speaking/Listening: discussions, conducting a survey, listening to radio or TV programmes, giving short presentation talks.
- Reading: books, newspapers, magazines, letters, tourist information
- Writing: making notes, letters to personal contacts or sources of official information, reports summarising researches.

Resources

- Library books: reference and/or literature
- Newspapers and magazines from the countries being studied
- TV and radio programmes, videos, films, slides
- Embassies of the appropriate countries
- Tourist information from travel agencies
- Personal contacts in countries

Lead-in activities

Stage-by-stage development suggestions

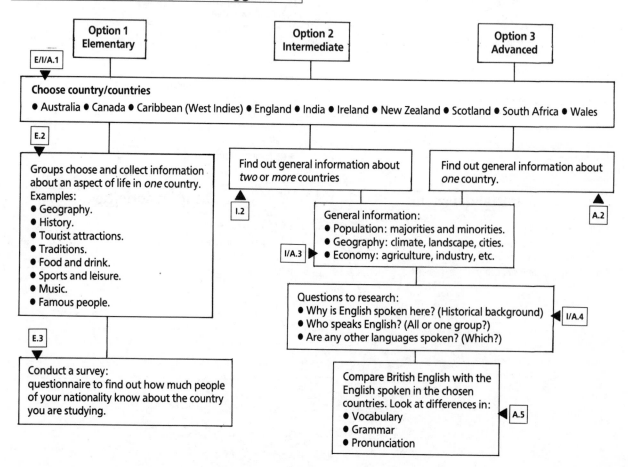

Option 1 Elementary

Option 2 Intermediate

Option 3 Advanced

E/I/A.1

Choose country/countries

● Australia ● Canada ● Caribbean (West Indies) ● England ● India ● Ireland ● New Zealand ● Scotland ● South Africa ● Wales

E.2

Groups choose and collect information about an aspect of life in *one* country.
Examples:
- Geography.
- History.
- Tourist attractions.
- Traditions.
- Food and drink.
- Sports and leisure.
- Music.
- Famous people.

Find out general information about *two* or *more* countries

I.2

Find out general information about *one* country.

A.2

I/A.3

General information:
- Population: majorities and minorities.
- Geography: climate, landscape, cities.
- Economy: agriculture, industry, etc.

Questions to research:
- Why is English spoken here? (Historical background)
- Who speaks English? (All or one group?)
- Are any other languages spoken? (Which?)

I/A.4

E.3

Conduct a survey:
questionnaire to find out how much people of your nationality know about the country you are studying.

Compare British English with the English spoken in the chosen countries. Look at differences in:
- Vocabulary
- Grammar
- Pronunciation

A.5

9 PRESSURE GROUPS

Suitability

Level: Advanced
Age: Secondary/Adult
Class: Students should have an interest in ideas, beliefs and causes

Project description

Basic: In this advanced project students investigate the work of special interest groups who are actively trying to influence government policy in Britain. A list of the names and addresses of some of these 'pressure groups' is given under the Resources heading below.

Variations: ● Students could do a comparative study of a pressure group in Britain and its equivalent in their own country.
● All groups could work on the same theme, e.g. the environment, or groups could work on different themes.

End product

A report, scrapbook or classroom display evaluating the work of the groups studied, including case studies looking in detail at particular pressure group campaigns.

Main activities

● Speaking/Listening: discussions, conducting a survey, giving short talks
● Reading: scan newspapers and magazines for reports of groups' past or present campaigns
● Writing: letters requesting information, summaries of pressure groups' beliefs, activities and methods

Resources

● Newspapers, magazines, books, TV, radio.
● Publicity material produced by pressure groups in your country.
● Publicity material produced by British pressure groups:

Environmental/Anti-nuclear groups:
1 Friends of the Earth (UK), 377 City Road, London EC1V 1NA.
2 Greenpeace, 30-31 Islington Green, London N1 8XE.
3 The Green Party, 10 Station Parade, Balham High Road, Balham, London SW12 9AZ.
4 Campaign for Nuclear Disarmament, 11 Goodwin Street, London N4 3HQ.

RACE RELATIONS
5 Commission for Racial Equality (CRE), Elliott House, 10/12 Allington Street, London SW1E 5EH.
6 Runnymede Trust Information Office, 37A Grays Inn Road, London WC1.
(Provides information on race relations in Britain and the European Community.)

THIRD WORLD ORGANISATIONS
7 Christian Aid, PO Box 1, London SW9 8BA.

8 Oxfam, Education Department, 274 Banbury Road, Oxford OX2 7DX.
9 Population Concern, 231 Tottenham Court Road, London W1P 9AE.
10 War on Want, 3 Castles House, 1 London Bridge Street, London SE1 9SG.

WOMEN'S ORGANISATIONS
11 Equal Opportunities Commission, Overseas House, Quay Street, Manchester M3 3HN.
12 Feminist Library and Information Centre, Hungerford House, Victoria Embankment, London WC2.
13 Rights of Women, 52 Featherstone Street, London EC1.

Lead-in activities

● Writing letters .... page 97
● Making notes .... page 92
● Giving a short talk .... page 79

Discussion points

▷ What is a pressure group?
▷ Why do these groups exist?
▷ Who belongs to them? (What kinds of people?)
▷ What kinds of issues are they mainly concerned with?
▷ Where do they get their money from?
▷ How are pressure groups regarded by governments and by the general public.

Types of groups	Issues and campaigns
● Environmental:	▷ Nuclear power
	▷ Alternative (natural) energy sources
	▷ Pollution (water, air and land)
	▷ Nature conservation
● Civil Liberties:	▷ Human rights (e.g. Amnesty International)
	▷ Race relations (e.g. immigrant rights)
	▷ Gay rights
	▷ Women's issues (e.g. equal opportunities)
	▷ Prison reform
	▷ Children's rights
	▷ Handicapped people
	▷ Old-age pensioners
● Third World:	▷ Famine relief (e.g. Ethiopia)
	▷ Disaster Aid (e.g. Sudan)
	▷ Intermediate (appropriate) technology
● Other Groups:	▷ Consumer groups (e.g. train and telephone users)
	▷ Animal rights (anti-vivisection; wildlife preservation – the protection of endangered species; anti-blood sports)
	▷ Employment (e.g. trade unions; employers' groups)

10 A NEWS DIARY

Suitability

Level: Intermediate/Advanced
Age: Secondary/Adult
Class: Students should have an interest in international current affairs

Project description

Basic: Students trace the development of a British news story and make notes about it in the form of a diary. The kind of stories chosen will depend on students' interests and on their level of English: intermediate classes, for example, might choose a crime story, or a sporting event, while more advanced students might prefer to follow a more complex or abstract story with political or social aspects. Depending on the particular stories chosen, this project may take between three and ten days to complete. Students need spend no more than one hour a day on their diaries.

Variations:
● If there are no suitable news stories taking place at the time you decide to do this project, students might be asked to find out about a personality currently in the news, e.g. a pop star, an actor, a politician, an infamous criminal, etc.

● Everyone in the class could follow the same story and make individual contributions to a class diary, or students might work in pairs or groups to produce separate diaries tracing the development of different stories.

● Different groups might follow stories from a variety of English-speaking countries, for example, USA, Canada, Australia, etc.

End product

A diary of events including the following:
● Note-form entries for each day that the story lasts

● Appropriate photographs and other illustrations

● Biographical details of the main personalities involved in the story

● Background information relevant to the story

● A final, single-page summary of the story, showing the development of events at a glance.

Main activities

● Speaking/Listening: discussions, listening to radio or TV news programmes
● Reading: newspapers and background books, proofreading
● Writing: making notes, recording events in diary form

Resources

● Current English-language newspapers and magazines. (Where these are difficult to get hold of, students may find information in newspapers in their own language.)
● BBC World Service news programmes. Of particular relevance will be:
  ▷ News about Britain
  ▷ Review of the British Press
● Radio and television programmes in your own country
● A selection of reference books

Lead-in activities

● Making notes .... page 92
● Using a dictionary .... page 103
● Giving a short talk .... page 79

Method

● Ideally, this project should arise naturally because a particularly interesting event takes place. Alternatively, students may find interesting stories by reading current British newspapers or by listening to a radio news programme about Britain.
● Follow the story as it develops by listening regularly to news summaries or by following the story in newspapers.
● Write up each day's news as it happens
● If students are working in pairs or groups, they should check and correct each other's written work.
● From time to time research background information. This may include:
  ▷ Finding out more about the place where the story is happening
  ▷ Researching historical background
  ▷ Finding out biographical information about personalities involved
● When diaries have been completed, individuals or groups should give a short talk to the rest of the class outlining the development of their story.
● This project might lead naturally on to a more in-depth study of an aspect of British life.

11 SPORT

Suitability

Level: All levels
Age: All ages
Class: No special requirements

Project description

A wide range of project options are possible under the general heading of 'Sport'. The suggestions should be adapted by teachers to suit the ability level and interests of their students. In order to justify this theme as an English-language project, the particular aspect of sport chosen should have a British or American connection. At the most elementary level, students might be expected to collect pictures of British or American sports personalities and write a little about them and their sport. At the other end of the scale, an advanced class might focus their attention on a sporting issue of current concern, such as *Drug-taking in Athletics*. It is clear that the organisation of and time allowed for the different sport project options will vary enormously, and for this reason the notes which follow are restricted to suggestions related to contents and student activities.

End product

The form of the end product will depend largely on the aspects of sport chosen by students, but might include the following:
- A scrapbook entitled, for example: *American Football*
- A diary tracing the fortunes of British or American individuals or teams in an international competition, for example *Wimbledon 199–*
- A demonstration of a game popular in Britain or America, but not played in the students' country, for example: a game of cricket
- A comparative study of the training facilities for young people in the USA and in your country
- A report on measures being taken in Britain or Canada to fight the use of drugs by athletes
- A class debate on the pros and cons of paying famous sports personalities large sums of money

Main activities

- Speaking/Listening: discussions, giving short talks, listening to radio and TV programmes, conducting a survey
- Reading: background information, newspaper reports
- Writing: making notes, writing letters requesting information
- Other: demonstrating games

Resources

- English-language newspapers and magazines
- Specialist sporting publications
- Reference books
- Video: demonstrating a particular sport or recording an important sporting event
- Sports programmes on radio or TV. (The World Service of the BBC has a regular worldwide sports programme called *Sports Roundup*)
- Personal contacts living in Britain or the USA, who could provide first-hand accounts or general information on particular sports.
- Information from sports clubs abroad or in your own country. Many countries have small clubs or associations which play minority sports. For example, there are a few cricket clubs in the Netherlands, and baseball clubs in many European countries.

Lead-in activities

(*Note:* Not all of these activities will be relevant to every type of sports project.)

Method

Content suggestions

- A single 'unknown' sport. Examples:
  ▷ American Football
  ▷ Baseball
  ▷ Rugby League/Rugby Union
  ▷ Cricket

- Comparative study of how a sport is organised in your country and in an English-speaking country. Examples:
  ▷ Football in your country and Britain
  ▷ Tennis in your country and the USA
  Other sports might include: golf, motor racing, athletics.

- Follow the fortunes of British or American teams or individuals in an important international sports event. Examples:
  ▷ The Olympic Games
  ▷ The World Cup (football)
  ▷ Wimbledon tennis
  ▷ A motor-racing Grand Prix
  ▷ European athletics

- Investigate current sporting issues. Examples:
  ▷ Drug-taking in athletics
  ▷ Amateur vs professional status
  ▷ Is boxing too violent?
  ▷ Should 'Blood Sports' be banned? (example: fox hunting)
  ▷ What should be done about hooliganism and violence at football matches?
  ▷ Is there too much sport on TV?
  ▷ How are young sports stars affected by fame?

Student activities

- Research all aspects of the sport: where it is played, the rules and equipment, famous teams or personalities.
  Write notes about the sport, collect relevant pictures, draw diagrams of positions.
  Groups give a talk or put on a demonstration game for the rest of the class.

- Exchange information with students in a school in Britain or the USA.
  Write to organisations abroad concerned with the sport.
  Write up results of research and present to the rest of the class: classroom displays and short talks.

- Listen to radio and TV programmes, read newspapers.
  Write a diary of events, or record progress on a wall chart in the classroom.
  Research and write profiles of sports personalities.
  Present findings to other students in the class.

- Research information from newspapers, books, sports authorities, etc.
  Write up notes, including relevant statistics.
  Conduct public opinion surveys and process results.
  Hold class discussion or debate and take vote on the issue in question.

FURTHER TOPIC SUGGESTIONS

1 ORGANISING A FUND-RAISING EVENT

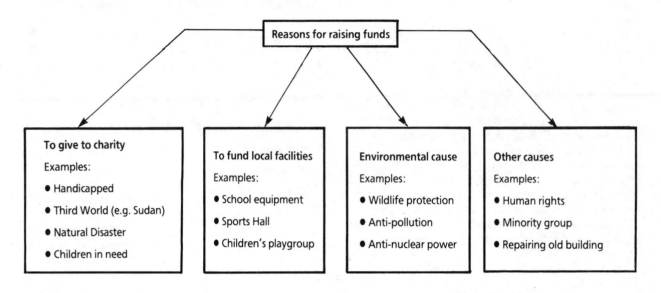

Reasons for raising funds

To give to charity

Examples:
- Handicapped
- Third World (e.g. Sudan)
- Natural Disaster
- Children in need

To fund local facilities

Examples:
- School equipment
- Sports Hall
- Children's playgroup

Environmental cause

Examples:
- Wildlife protection
- Anti-pollution
- Anti-nuclear power

Other causes

Examples:
- Human rights
- Minority group
- Repairing old building

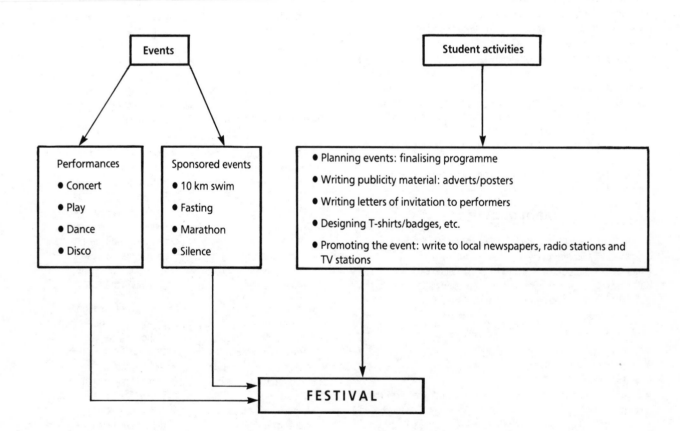

Events

Performances
- Concert
- Play
- Dance
- Disco

Sponsored events
- 10 km swim
- Fasting
- Marathon
- Silence

Student activities

- Planning events: finalising programme
- Writing publicity material: adverts/posters
- Writing letters of invitation to performers
- Designing T-shirts/badges, etc.
- Promoting the event: write to local newspapers, radio stations and TV stations

FESTIVAL

2 PRODUCING A RADIO PROGRAMME

(*Note:* This is a variation of the newspaper project, which involves students in the preparation of spoken as well as written language. All items should have a British or American connection.)

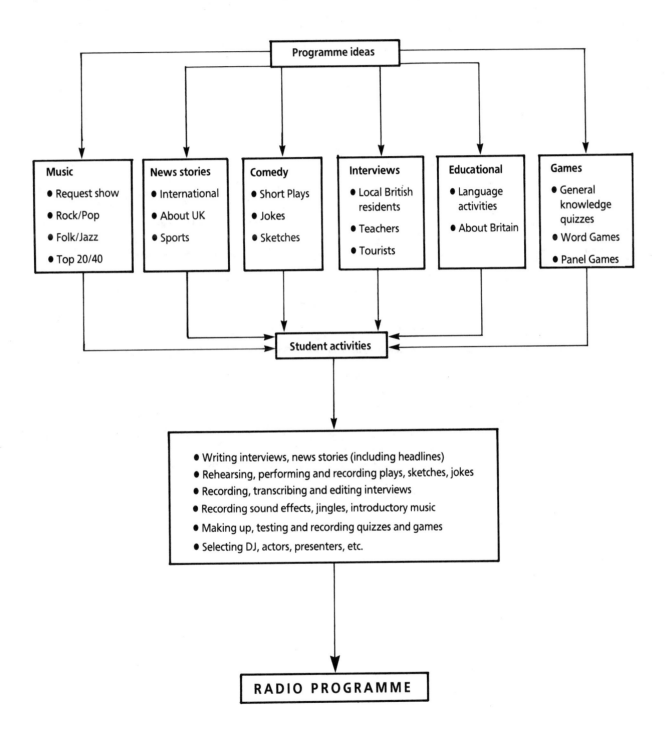

Programme ideas

Music
- Request show
- Rock/Pop
- Folk/Jazz
- Top 20/40

News stories
- International
- About UK
- Sports

Comedy
- Short Plays
- Jokes
- Sketches

Interviews
- Local British residents
- Teachers
- Tourists

Educational
- Language activities
- About Britain

Games
- General knowledge quizzes
- Word Games
- Panel Games

Student activities

- Writing interviews, news stories (including headlines)
- Rehearsing, performing and recording plays, sketches, jokes
- Recording, transcribing and editing interviews
- Recording sound effects, jingles, introductory music
- Making up, testing and recording quizzes and games
- Selecting DJ, actors, presenters, etc.

RADIO PROGRAMME

3 BRITISH CUSTOMS

(*Note:* This project involves students investigating traditional British customs. Information about the more historical traditions may be found in books, whereas modern customs are best researched through contact with British people. If such contact is not a practical possibility, it would be best to direct students away from 'modern customs'.)

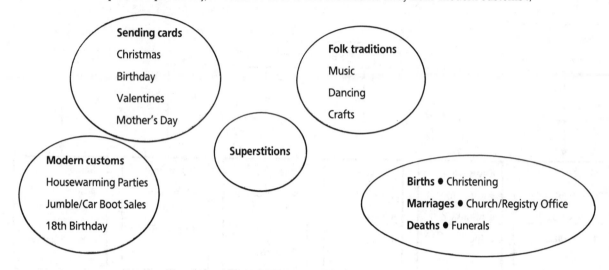

Sending cards

Christmas

Birthday

Valentines

Mother's Day

Folk traditions

Music

Dancing

Crafts

Modern customs

Housewarming Parties

Jumble/Car Boot Sales

18th Birthday

Superstitions

Births ● Christening

Marriages ● Church/Registry Office

Deaths ● Funerals

Traditional celebrations

January	● New Year celebrations (Scotland/Northern England)
February	● Valentine cards
March/April	● Easter
May	● May Day celebrations
June	● Midsummer Fires (Scotland/Cornwall/Northumberland)
July	● Swan Upping (River Thames)
September	● Harvest Festivals
October	● Hallowe'en
November	● Guy Fawkes Night with fireworks and bonfires
December	● Christmas Eve/Christmas Day/Boxing Day

Student activities

- Research: library books/magazines/newspapers
- Writing: notes/short descriptions
- Contacting British families
- Questioning British people in your country
- Comparing celebrations in your country and in Britain e.g. Christmas
- Comparing superstitions

4 THE FAMILY

(*Note:* This is a comparative study of the current state of the family as a social institution in your country and in Britain or USA. To make this project effective, you will need to make contact with British or American people via a link school, a town-twinning organisation or personal contacts.

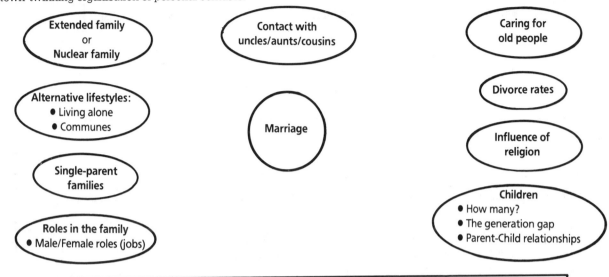

Student activities

- Researching, drawing and labelling family trees.
- Survey: writing and sending questionnaires to British people.
- Interviewing British/American people in your country.
- Reading newspapers (e.g. divorce figures/male-female roles).
- Summarising information in charts, graphs, tables of figures, etc.
- Discussions: comparisons between your country and Britain/predicting likely future trends.

5 POLITICS IN BRITAIN

(*Note:* This is suitable for an advanced class of students with an interest in political matters.)

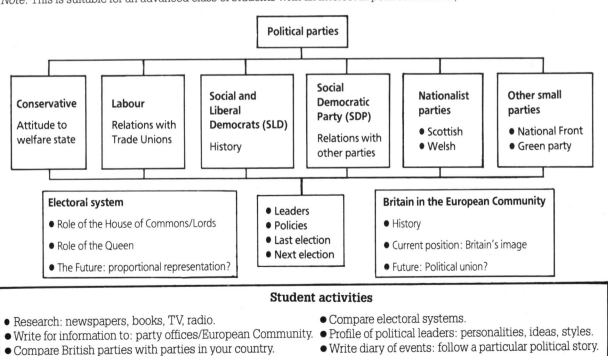

Student activities

- Research: newspapers, books, TV, radio.
- Write for information to: party offices/European Community.
- Compare British parties with parties in your country.
- Compare electoral systems.
- Profile of political leaders: personalities, ideas, styles.
- Write diary of events: follow a particular political story.

6 LINKS BETWEEN YOUR COUNTRY AND BRITAIN

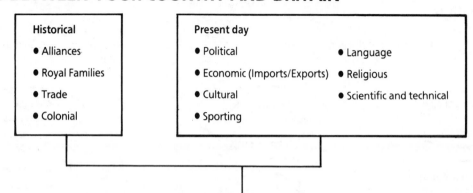

Historical
- Alliances
- Royal Families
- Trade
- Colonial

Present day
- Political
- Economic (Imports/Exports)
- Cultural
- Sporting
- Language
- Religious
- Scientific and technical

Student activities

- Give students a choice of looking at historical or present-day links.
- Write for information e.g. embassies, business organisations, European Community, etc.
- Compare accounts of historical periods or events as described by British historians and historians from your country.
- Study how English and your language have affected each other.
- Survey: the number of tourists going from your country to Britain and vice-versa.
- Read and write about past and present sports meetings between your country and Britain (e.g. football/tennis/athletics).

7 IMPRESSIONS OF BRITAIN

(*Notes:* 1 This project is only possible if the majority of students in the class have visited Britain or another English-speaking country.
2 Students might each work on an individual project, and only work with other students during a proofreading activity.)

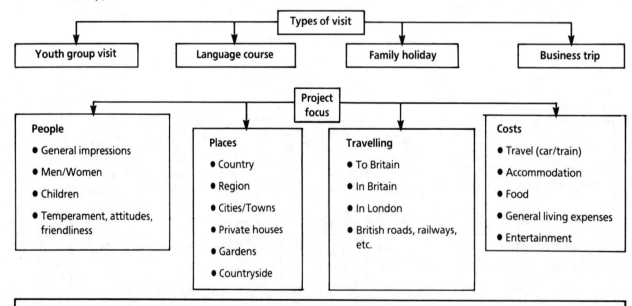

Types of visit

| Youth group visit | Language course | Family holiday | Business trip |

Project focus

People
- General impressions
- Men/Women
- Children
- Temperament, attitudes, friendliness

Places
- Country
- Region
- Cities/Towns
- Private houses
- Gardens
- Countryside

Travelling
- To Britain
- In Britain
- In London
- British roads, railways, etc.

Costs
- Travel (car/train)
- Accommodation
- Food
- General living expenses
- Entertainment

Student activities

- Writing: a diary of events/impressions of the country and its people before and after the visit.
- Comparing an aspect of Britain with your own country.
- Write letters requesting information from the tourist information office for the region or town visited. (Addresses: see Appendix, page 108)

8 RACIAL MINORITIES IN BRITAIN

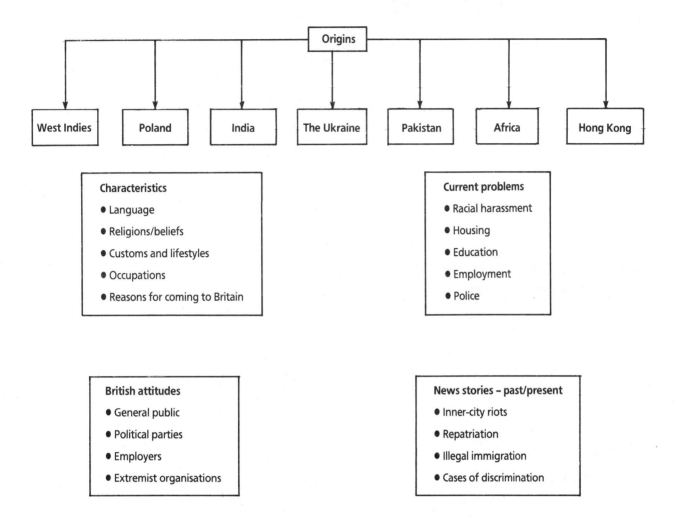

Origins

- West Indies
- Poland
- India
- The Ukraine
- Pakistan
- Africa
- Hong Kong

Characteristics
- Language
- Religions/beliefs
- Customs and lifestyles
- Occupations
- Reasons for coming to Britain

Current problems
- Racial harassment
- Housing
- Education
- Employment
- Police

British attitudes
- General public
- Political parties
- Employers
- Extremist organisations

News stories – past/present
- Inner-city riots
- Repatriation
- Illegal immigration
- Cases of discrimination

Student activities

- Research: books, newspapers, magazines, TV/Radio programmes.

- Write questionnaire about attitudes. Send to British contacts.

- Write for information to Race Relations organisations:

  Commission for Racial Equality (CRE), Elliott House, 10/12 Allington St., London SW1 5EH
  Runnymede Trust Information Office, 37A Grays Inn Road, London WC1

- Compare the situation of minority groups in Britain with equivalent groups in your country.

- Discussion of causes of problems and possible solutions.

This chapter describes the project work experiences of teachers in different parts of the world.
- Part 1 contains outlines of four projects devised by teachers.
- Part 2 consists of extracts from teachers' reports on some of the full and framework projects in Chapter 3 of this book. This part is subdivided in Teachers' reactions and Students' reactions to project work.
- Part 3 contains sample project work produced by students.

PART ONE: TEACHERS' OWN PROJECTS

1 TEACHING ENGLISH THROUGH ENGLISH: A VIDEO PROJECT, Patricio Bracamonte

Students' situation

Thirteen young adults: fourth level students at a teacher training college in Santiago, Chile.

Level of English

Students were preparing for the Cambridge First Certificate examination.

Objectives

1 To make students use English language in real situations.

2 To provide students with situations in which they could use language more creatively.

3 To familiarise students with video as a teaching aid.

4 To help students develop management skills.
The end product was a TV programme, recorded on video.

Stages

The project was planned in four stages:

1 the planning and writing of scripts,

2 the recording and presentation of work,

3 the preparation of a worksheet: tasks for exploitation of the video with either first or second level students at the Teacher Training College,

4 microteaching and testing of materials, and final evaluation by the same group of students.

Project description

As soon as the idea was presented, the students reacted enthusiastically, and although constraints such as tests, timetables, bad colds and long recording sessions were always present, their enthusiasm never waned. The first stage was for the students to decide in groups what they wanted to do, who wanted to do what and the order of the programme. Because we had only one video recorder, we wouldn't be able to do any editing, so the programme would have to be recorded in the order in which it was to appear. The final programme decided on was as follows:
- A news bulletin: reports on the cafeteria, a museum, and the Students' Union.
- A ballet performance
- An interview
- A sketch
It was also decided that each part of the programme should have a presenter.

For the piece of news on the museum, a visit to the Natural History Museum was planned, and the students prepared a brochure for visiting tourists. Once the brochure was finished, it was sent to the Director of the Museum who decided to adopt it officially.

Groups were also formed to help the 'actors': sound, visuals, make-up, costumes, etc.

For the interview section of the programme, contact was made with a local representative of the British Council. The group in charge had to meet the representative, show him our studio, and offer him a cup of coffee after the interview. This gave our students the chance of speaking with a native speaker in a real situation.

Once finished, the programme was viewed several times by fourth level students and the teachers in charge, who all appeared to enjoy it.

Evaluation

At the end of the Video Project, the students were asked to evaluate their work. They were given five questions:
1 **Do you think the project was a valuable experience? Why? Why not? Consider language and other, extra-linguistic aspects.**
   a *Students referred to the project with adjectives like 'very interesting', 'demanding', 'most valuable', 'great', and 'tiring'.*
   b *They said it was a different way of learning and an opportunity to practise what they had learnt during the previous two years.*
   c *They felt that they had shared responsibilities and that the contact with classmates and teachers had been something positive.*

2 Did you feel at any point that the project was just a way of not doing 'conventional' classes?

Almost everyone's answer was 'No, of course not.' One student mentioned there should have been 'conventional' classes running parallel.

3 Are you satisfied with the part you took in the project? If not, what would you have liked to do?

Everybody answered 'Yes' except for one girl who was not happy with what she had done in the sketch.

4 What aspects of planning and presentation could be improved?

 a Some students thought it was not the best time of the year. It would have been better at the beginning of the term.

 b Two said it needed more planning.

 c Two said it needed better organisation because, during the planning stage, some groups finished earlier than others. As a solution they suggested a practice examination.

5 Did the project interfere with your preparation for the First Certificate Examination or with your performance in other subjects?

The answer was 'No', except for one student who mentioned a translation test.

Conclusion

I would like to emphasise that in this amateurish production the *process* was much more important than the *product*, as it was carried out in English. The group worked as a team as never before, and both teachers and students found it a rewarding experience in terms of teaching and learning, as well as in terms of social contact.

2: TALENT SHOW, Barbara Kruchin

Students' situation:

Young adults learning English at a private language school in Porto Alegre, Brazil.

Level of English

Early elementary.

Length of time taken

2 - 2½ months.

Aim of project

To present a play: *Cinderella*.
The end product was a 15-minute sketch presented at a school party and performed entirely by students.

Stages:

1 Arouse students' interest by describing the talent show and mentioning the prize: one month's free language tuition for one person. (15 minutes)

2 Students choose or write a play. The teacher helped with ideas. (2-3 hours)

3 Rehearsals: the teachers gave help with vocabulary, pronunciation and intonation. (8-10 hours)

4 Encouraging and reassuring the students just before the presentation of the play; helping with make-up, costumes, etc.

Teacher's comments

1 The main benefit of this project was 'the idea that at any level students can use language communicatively - I don't mean to do a role play, where the teacher expects students to practise certain language points, but a lot freer than that.'

2 What was particularly successful was 'the quality of the theatrical work and language production.' I was pleased that 'early elementary students could do *Cinderella* and that they did it very well from a linguistic point of view.'

3 This project 'made students aware that language was something alive, fun, creative, something that one can play with. In all aspects the language was a lot more realistic than it (normally) is in the classroom.'

3: THE PROBLEM OF APARTHEID IN SOUTH AFRICA, Marciano Palazzo

Students' situation

14-year-olds at a state secondary school in Foggia, Italy.

Level of English

Intermediate/Advanced.

Aim of project

To give students the opportunity to practise the four skills, mainly understanding, interpreting and speaking. The end product was an article for the class newspaper.

Total time taken

Five hours.

Beginnings

The pupils showed an interest in apartheid after reading about Gandhi's life in South Africa and after watching a TV programme on the same subject.

Students worked in groups on different aspects of the same subject.

Stages

1 Presentation of the subject: pupils watched pre-recorded video material; the first part of the film *Gandhi*, and a documentary about apartheid. (1 hour)

2 Presentation of materials: the students were given photocopies from English newspapers and magazines. They scanned the articles and underlined points that would be useful for the report. (1 hour)

3 Students discussed the points they had picked out and began arranging an order of paragraphs for the report. They found and wrote down, in note form, the points which recurred in the texts. They then selected appropriate photographs. (1 hour)

4 The class discussed the content with the teacher, and decided on the final order and form of their report. (1 hour)

5 The report was typed and photocopied for the school newspaper. Each group gave an oral presentation of the aspect of the topic that they had covered. (1 hour)

Teacher's Comments

1 On the teacher's role in the project:
'First, that of resource - I procured books, magazines, newspapers and videos about the subject. Then an adviser and consultant - I helped students to select the most important points from the many chosen.'

2 Correcting students' English:
'I corrected them mainly when they used irregular verbs as regular ones, and when they used the interrogative and negative forms without *do* or *did*, especially when they were asking each other questions. In addition I checked their ability to understand the magazine articles.'

3 'The students realised that learning by doing satisfies their need to acquire fluency, since it gives the opportunity for free communication.'

4 'I was particularly pleased by the co-operation between the teacher and the class, and between myself and teachers of other subjects*. I appreciated the opportunity to give pupils new information about the outside world as part of their language work.'

(* *Note:* History, geography and religious studies teachers participated in this project.)

4: CLASS NEWSPAPER, Jose Molina

Students' situation

Twelve students, aged 17-19, at a state secondary school in Lucena, Spain.

Level of English

Intermediate.

Total time taken

Eight hours.

Aim of project

To expose students to English newspapers and to get them to summarise a weekend's news.

The end project was a class newspaper called *Daily COU-B Mail*.

Beginnings

'I had this idea in mind since the beginning of the second term and I knew there was a topic in the coursebook about the press. Besides this, some of the students were working on a school newspaper in Spanish.'

Stages

1 Introduction to the topic 'The English Press', using examples of popular and quality newspapers. The class discussed and compared newspapers in Spain and Britain. (1 hour)

2 I (teacher) gave out newspapers bought in Cordoba. The class looked at them and commented on the main news items. (1 hour)

3 After skimming and scanning at home, students each chose two pieces of news and brought them into class. The group agreed on a format and a news story was allocated to each student. (2 hours)

4 Students wrote summarised versions of their news stories at home. They brought them into class and corrected them together. (2 hours)

5 We started to work on the agreed newspaper format, decided on headlines and looked for jokes to fill the empty spaces. (1 hour)

6 We finished and published the first Class English newspaper. (1 hour)

Teacher's Comments

1 On the teacher's role in the project:
'I've got to admit I played an important role in directing, organising, making photocopies, etc. A group of good students also helped most of the time. I involved myself in discussions, but not in the decisions, which were taken by the students themselves.'

2 Correcting students' English:
'I didn't have to correct the students' English very often, because they had had practice in summarising.'

3 'What was most pleasing was that students were reading and understanding authentic articles without knowing all the vocabulary. I was also impressed by the "real newspaper" appearance of the end product.'

4 The students were pleased about 'being able to do in English something that would be quite easy for them in Spanish.'

5 Problems:
'Finding samples of all the English newspapers published at weekends.'
'At the beginning the students were overwhelmed by the number of pages written in English. They wanted to look up all the words they didn't know; this was something I didn't allow.'

(*Note:* This is one of the many variations on the popular 'newspaper' project. For other ideas, turn to Framework Project 3, News about your Country, page 45.)

PART TWO: REACTIONS TO PROJECT WORK

These comments are taken from reports returned by teachers who tested some of the Projects and Lead-in activities included in this book.

1 TEACHERS' REACTIONS

1.1 Subject matter

'It gave me an insight into what the students found interesting as opposed to what I think they find interesting.' (PA - England)

'It's the first time I've worked on a project that consisted of the collection and processing of purely factual information. I find it limiting and still prefer projects that depend on students' creative or imaginative abilities. (LA - Spain)

1.2 Organisation and timing

'Take more time, and don't do projects at the end of term.' (JM - Spain)

'I think I could improve the results if I worked with a reduced group on six or seven consecutive days.' (LFR - Spain)

'One thing I've found about project work is that however badly I manage it, whatever blunders I make, my students always come back begging for more.' (LA - Spain)

'I think it's very important to explain to students the basic objectives and benefits of project work, so they realise it's not a lark, non-serious entertainment, or an excuse for the teacher to do as little as possible.' (LA - Spain)

'I think time is the enemy - we only had six periods in class to get everything together.' (SB - Switzerland)

1.3 Teacher's role

'The only problem I had was how to curb over-ambitious plans, knowing when to let students get carried away and when to step in and control.' (LA - Spain)

'My role in the project was "consultative" - but on the whole I got a bit bored as I seemed so redundant! I point out that this was an exceptional class from the point of view of group dynamics.' (LA - Spain)

'I tried to be non-directive, but because of the time limitations, I had to provoke some decisions. (SB - Switzerland)

'I tried not to be too directive. However, because of their previous experience at school, etc., most French adults prefer directive interventions from their teachers.' (JR - France)

2 STUDENTS' REACTIONS

'The students realised the importance of being informed, and an old idea that one of my teachers at university used to tell us "contact English everyday, it doesn't matter if it is a comic or a newspaper". It was good to relax in groups, sharing ideas.' (JFM - Spain)

'Although students tried to speak English throughout the project work in class, this did not always work out.' (JM - Spain)

'They were very ready to collaborate. I think they are now much more fond of English.' (LFR - Spain)

'The project motivated students so much that it made them not only work by themselves, but also be competitive in the use of language and, what's better, in the communicative skills. The most outstanding aspect was to see students working actively. The most successful was to discover that the very slow ones were working with enthusiasm and took an active part in the project.' (PH - Spain)

'There was some difficulty at the very beginning of the project. When it was presented, it was hard for students to understand the aim of the project.' (PH - Spain)

'Some groups worked totally independently, but others found it difficult to go ahead without a check up from the teacher. This is due to their age (14-17 years old) and the training they receive at school.' (LA - Spain)

'They have developed confidence in the manipulation of the language both oral and written, and were very proud of the booklet they finally produced. They got so involved they put in extra hours outside the class when previously the very mention of homework provoked outbursts of horror. For students working in a non-English-speaking environment, maximum exposure to English in whatever form is of paramount importance.' (LA - Spain)

'Students took over and organised the final product. Although we ignored a large part of the syllabus, exam results were higher than average. (LA - Spain)

'Students saw that English is a highly important commodity - nearly a necessity - in the workforce, and that school is still the best place to learn for most of them. There was a co-operative effort among groups who (usually) tend to ignore each other.' (SB - Switzerland)

'The students saw the project uniquely as a means of improving their spoken and written English. They saw no social importance whatsoever.' (JR - France)

'It helped the students to make progress in developing communicative skills. They found the work interesting, useful, and "such fun".' (TG - Bulgaria)

PART 3: SAMPLES OF STUDENT PROJECT WORK

EXAMPLE 1

English Language Survey
(Full Project 2 - page 20)

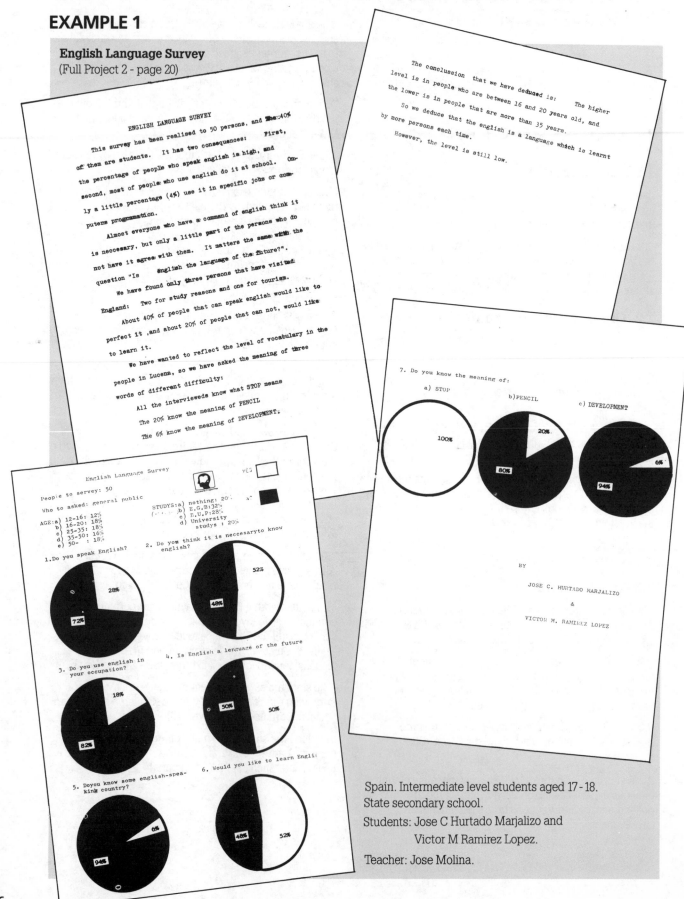

ENGLISH LANGUAGE SURVEY

This survey has been realised to 50 persons, and the 40% of them are students. It has two consequences: First, the percentage of people who speak english is high, and most of people who use english do it at school. On second, ly a little percentage (4%) use it in specific jobs or computers programmation.

Almost everyone who have a command of english think it is neccesary, but only a little part of the persons who do not have it agree with them. It matters the same with the question "Is english the language of the future?".

We have found only three persons that have visited England: Two for study reasons and one for tourism.

About 40% of people that can speak english would like to perfect it, and about 20% of people that can not, would like to learn it.

We have wanted to reflect the level of vocabulary in the people in Lucena, so we have asked the meaning of three words of different difficulty:

All the intervieweds know what STOP means
The 20% know the meaning of PENCIL
The 6% know the meaning of DEVELOPMENT.

The conclussion that we have deduced is: The higher level is in people who are between 16 and 20 years old, and the lower is in people that are more than 35 years. So we deduce that the english is a language which is learnt by more persons each time. However, the level is still low.

7. Do you know the meaning of:

a) STOP   b) PENCIL   c) DEVELOPMENT
100%   20% / 80%   6% / 94%

BY

JOSE C. HURTADO MARJALIZO
&
VICTOR M. RAMIREZ LOPEZ

English Language Survey

People to servey: 50
Who to asked: general public   STUDYS:a) nothing: 20%
AGE:a) 12-16: 12%   b) E.G.B:32%
     b) 16-20: 18%   c) E.U.P:28%
     c) 25-35: 18%   d) University
     d) 35-50: 16%   studys : 20%
     e) 50- : 18%

1.Do you speak English?   2. Do you think it is neccesary to know english?
28% / 72%   52% / 48%

3. Do you use english in your occupation?   4. Is English a lenguage of the future
18% / 82%   50% / 50%

5. Do you know some english-speaking country?   6. Would you like to learn English
6% / 94%   48% / 52%

Spain. Intermediate level students aged 17 - 18.
State secondary school.
Students: Jose C Hurtado Marjalizo and
          Victor M Ramirez Lopez.
Teacher: Jose Molina.

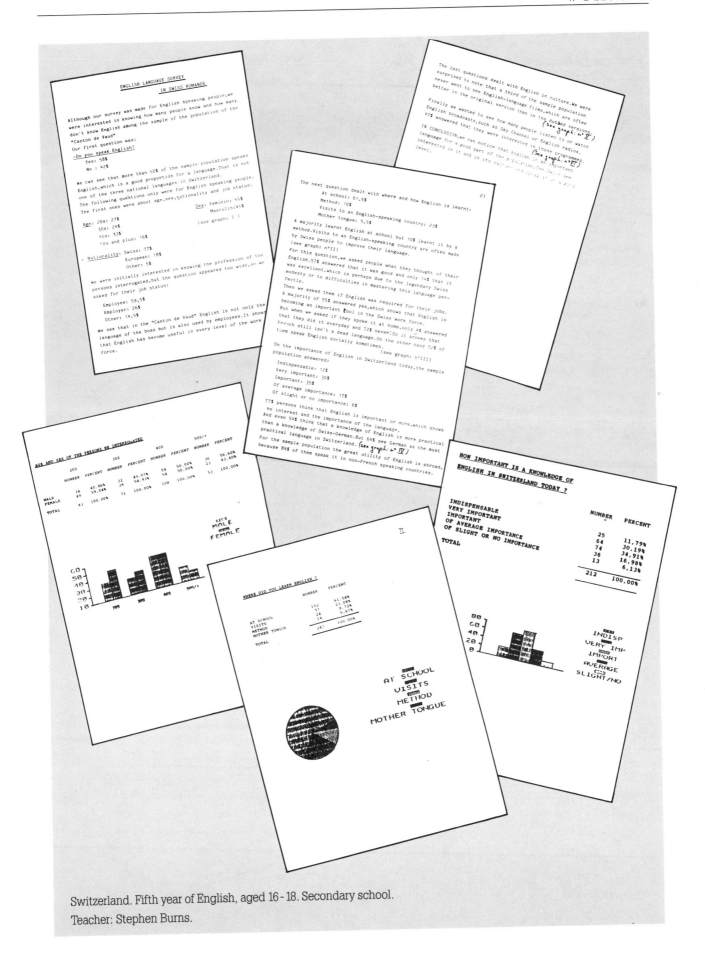

Switzerland. Fifth year of English, aged 16 - 18. Secondary school.
Teacher: Stephen Burns.

EXAMPLE 2

Producing a School Guide
(variation on Full Project 3 - page 25)

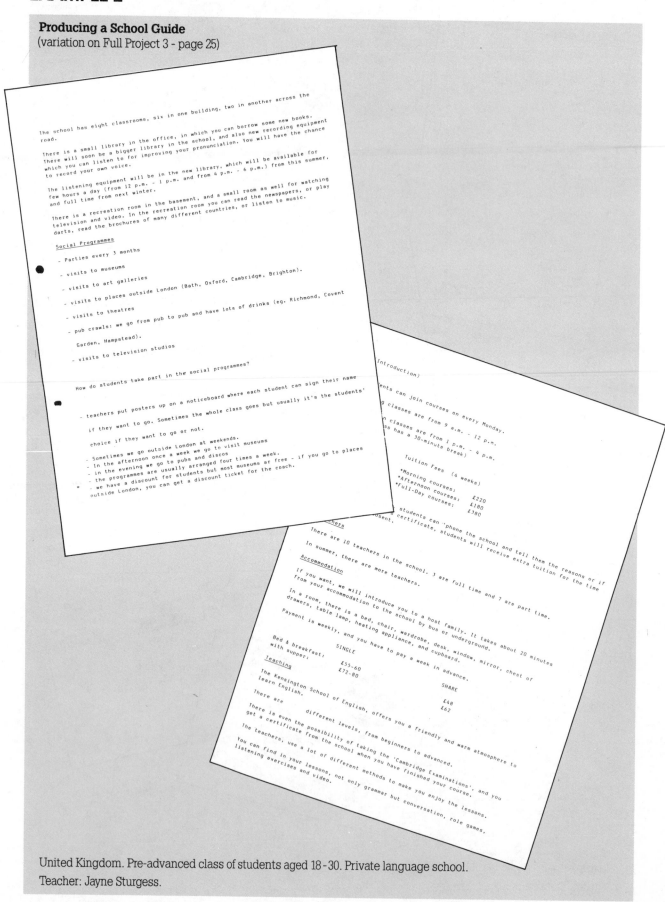

United Kingdom. Pre-advanced class of students aged 18-30. Private language school.
Teacher: Jayne Sturgess.

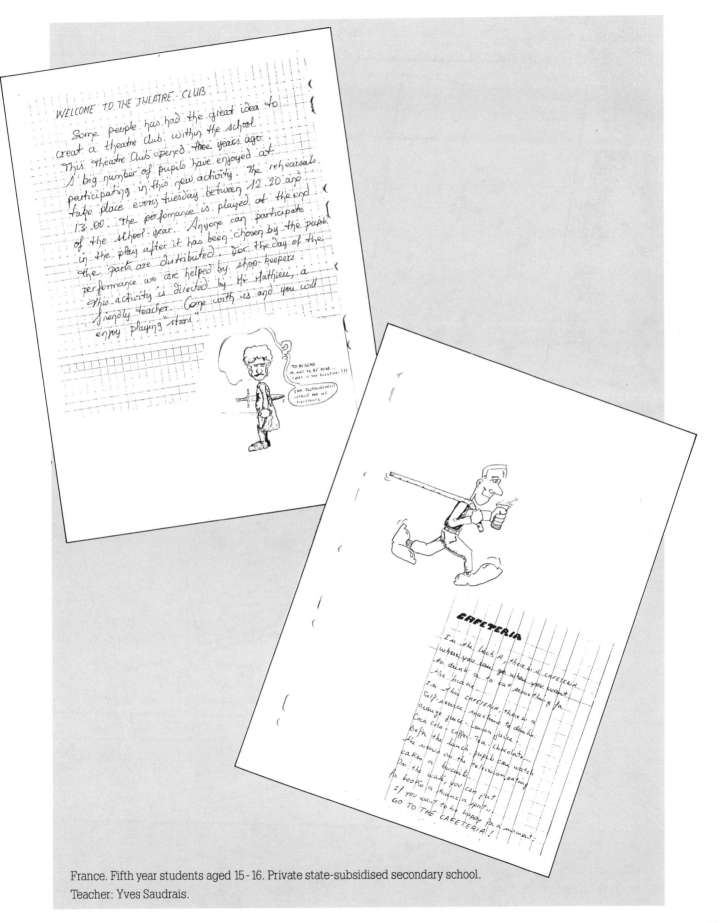

France. Fifth year students aged 15 - 16. Private state-subsidised secondary school.
Teacher: Yves Saudrais.

EXAMPLE 3

Producing a Newspaper
(variation on Framework Project 3 - page 45)

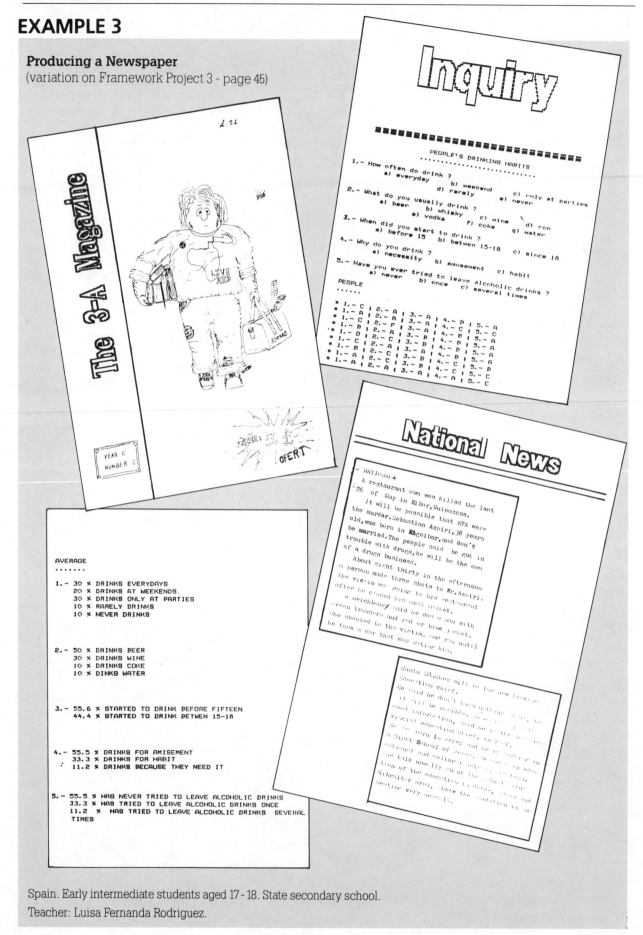

Spain. Early intermediate students aged 17 - 18. State secondary school.

Teacher: Luisa Fernanda Rodriguez.

Daily COU B Mail

THURSDAY, MARCH 26, 1987 20p

to be won
Supermatch—Page 34

Russia rolls out red carpet

NEW-BROOM Soviet leader Mikhail Gorbachev has ordered remarkable Comradski treatment for Mrs Thatcher when she visits Russia at the weekend.

Mrs Thatcher intends to sound out the Russians about the pace and direction of arms control, raise human rights issues and drum up contracts and Soviets orders for British industry.

But one cloud appeared over the trip yesterday. Russia's General Yuri Lebedev warned that Mrs Thatcher will have to scrap Polaris if she wants cuts in Soviet conventional forces in Europe.

Mr Gorbachev believes that her calls for the obstacles to peace and arms reduction.

Details of her historic trip were described by diplomats as "spectacular".

By Leles Tirado

CHERNOBYL'S BOMB

It was the disaster without frontiers—a tragedy whose deadly effects will still be felt all over Western well into the next century.

The experts are all agreed that hundreds of people will die of cancer as a result of the Chernobyl nuclear accident eleven months ago.

The study by the National Radiological Protection Board at Harwell, Oxfordshire, says the findings are "middle of the range".

The horror of Chernobyl is grim proof that deadly radioactive fall out is no respecter of national boundaries.

The tragic truth is that there is no escape from its undeadly effects.

The pollution is already here and there is nothing we can do about.

By Mª Angeles Lozano

THATCHER PLANS WALK-ABOUTS ON MOSCOW VISIT

MRS THATCHER is planning walk-abouts to meet Russian people in the streets shops and their homes during her five-day visit to the Soviet Union.

The Soviet authorities have arranged what the Government describe as several "spectacular" outing for the Prime Minister, as well as full-day of talks with Mr Gorbachev the Soviet leader.

KREMLIN TALKS

The main working day of the visit will be Monday, when Mrs Thatcher will have two rounds of talks with Mr Gorbachev in the Kremlin.

On her arrival on Saturday evening she will have an official welcome in the Kremlin

REAGAN READY TO TURN DOWN KINNOCK'S DEFENCE POLICY

In Europe to be reduced will be voiced to Mr Neil Kinnock on his short visit to the United States. Firm rejection of his party's non nuclear stance from president Reagan, said the American European Community Association. Mr Reagan think that is unnacceptable to Nato (it was confirmed yesterday). It belives that because the d decision to deploy cruise was taken by Nato. Tomorrow's meeting between Mr Kinnock and the president takes place against the background. Mr Reagan is determined to resist, to cut the budget by reducing. Mr Kinnock will meet Mr Bill Bradley and Mr John Tower, chairman of the Irangate board of inquiry.

by James Mellado

EQUAL PAY VICTORY FOR BATTLING RENE

Judges overturn tribunal ruling on women's wages

EQUAL PAY VICTORY FOR BATTLING RENE

By Araceli Gómez

Rene Bickstone won yesterday a mayor victory in her battle for equal pay. Thousands of working women will have joined her in celebrating the ruling of the Apeal Court judges that she has the right to claim equal pay with men for doing work of equal value.

Rene, who works for Freemans mail order company in Peterborogh tribunals which both ruled that she could not two industrial wages which made workers doing different jobs. But their ruling was overturned by the Appeal Court which made legal history by applying European Community law. As a result of this case many other women could bring claim of equal pay.

Spain. Intermediate level students aged 17 - 19. State secondary school.
Teacher: Jose Molina.

EXAMPLE 4

The American Influence on your Way of Life
(Full Project 4 -page 30)

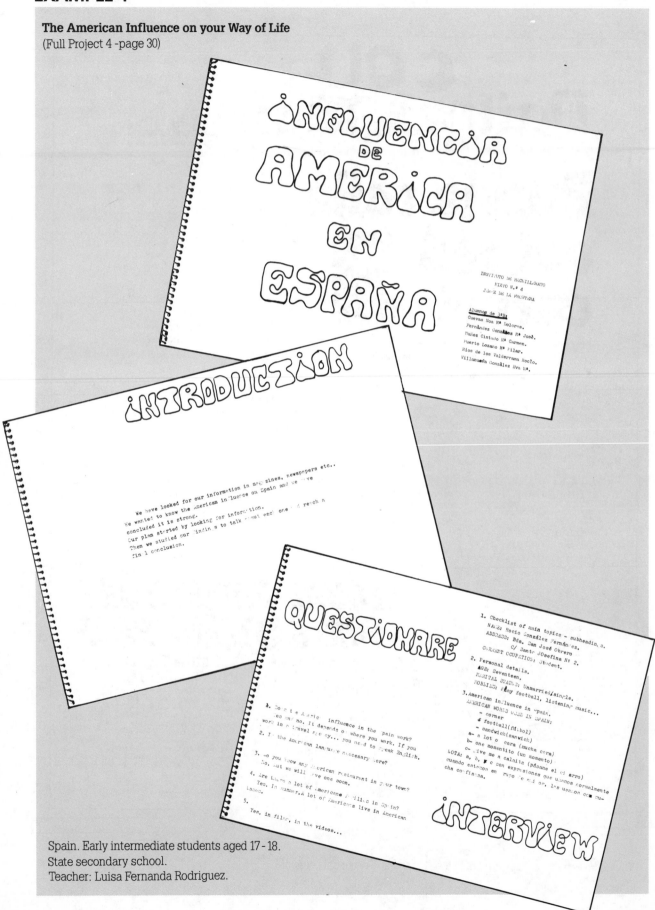

Spain. Early intermediate students aged 17 - 18.
State secondary school.
Teacher: Luisa Fernanda Rodriguez.

INTRODUCTORY NOTES

For general suggestions about these activities refer to Chapter 1, Section 7, page 5.

1 GIVING A SHORT TALK

Activity 1

1 Explain the aim of this activity and pre-teach these words: *subject*, *heading*, *keyword*.
2 Set a time limit for these talks (e.g. 2 minutes) and hand out photocopied sheets.
3 Students work through Activity 1, stages 1-4, using the examples as models for the preparation of their own talks.
4 In stage 5, do not interrupt students' talks but, when they have finished, comment on the effectiveness of their presentation.

Activity 2

1 In this activity, students practise talking about a subject that has been chosen for them.
2 Once the subjects have been decided, students should prepare their talks as in Activity 1. These talks should last one minute.

Further activities

These two additional activities are suitable for more advanced students. Although they are both games, they will give students practice in speaking off-the-cuff.

2 PROOFREADING

Choose the appropriate proofreading exercise for your class and make sure students understand what they have to do.

Elementary

1 Corrected version:

My name is Astrid. I am going to **be nineteen years** old on 26th **November**. I live in France. I don't speak English very well, so I **have come** to England to learn the language, because I think English is very **important** for **finding** a job (because I have already passed my **secretarial** exam).

I live on a **farm** near Ardeligh with **a pleasant/kind** family and I look **after** 2 **children aged four** years old and **two** years old.

I **have been** here **for** only six weeks, so I **can't** say much about life in England. For example the people I meet at the farm are kind and they try to **talk to me**. (The dictionary is **useful** also.)

4 Corrected version:

British Customs and Traditions

Television:
Always stupid shows and **soap operas**. Sometimes there **are** good things like the NEWS.

Eating and Drinking:
English people **don't** say **anything** when they **start to eat**. They have **a** special **way of putting their knives and forks down** after they **have** finished **their** meal.

They don't drink water and **always** put a glass of wine **on** the table.

Shops:
Shops usually **open** at 9.00 o'clock in the morning and **close** at 5.30 in the **evening**. **Some** of **the** shops **stay** open until 8 **or** 10 **o'clock**, like the big **shops**. They have **big supermarkets** for **things** which **they use daily**.

Intermediate

1 Corrected version:

When I arrived **in** England I found **everything different**. The **towns** were very **quiet** and the houses very **nice**. **People in Spain have houses like these outside the city to visit for holidays or at weekends.**

The food and **mealtimes are very** different too. **English people are always** very **polite**, but **not** really friendly because **they** are very **reserved**. **For that reason it** is difficult to **make** English friends.

English people are very **self-centred**, because **they think** that they are the best in the world and **that** their **country has** the best things: **there is nothing good in other countries.**

7 Corrected version:

I'm a 16-year-old girl and I've got a big problem: I'm studying for my exams and I want to study hard, but I have got **a** lot of **friends** and I love going out with them. What **can** I do to study and **enjoy myself at** the same time? Thanks for your answer.

*Well, I think that you ought to **make a study plan** and after **doing your** homework you could go out with your group of friends.*

Hello!

I'm a pastry-cook and I would **like to** know what **I can** do **to get rid of** the spots of chocolate **on** my clothes. Thank you very much.

*It's very easy: with **warm** water and a good clothes cleaner. If this isn't enough you **should** take your clothes to a **professional** cleaner.*

Advanced

1 Corrected version:

At the moment easy communications between countries allow **the introduction** of new **customs** and **new relationships** between different **ways** of life. Developing countries depend **for their progress** on developed countries, and they imitate developed countries **as if they were symbols** of progress. It is a fact that at **the** moment Anglo-Saxon **countries** in general, **particularly** the United **States, are regarded as** the most developed **countries.**

Life in our country**,** Spain**,** like **life** in **other countries,** appears to be influenced by this civilization**. The** English language is **absolutely essential in/for** some jobs**. Scientific** or new **technological** vocabulary is full of English words**; a** lot of films are made by English or American directors**. Every day** the number of multi-nationals in our country **is increasing.**

Every day electoral **campaigns** seem more **American,** and perhaps **every day** we eat more chips and chicken or hamburgers. Is **this** a new sign of colonization? **Are** hamburgers **replacing** Spanish food?

5 Corrected version:

English Language

English is **spoken by** more **than** 350 **million** people and it **has a** great influence **at the** moment, because **it** is considered **to be** the first **language** in the world. It's **spoken** in Great Britain, USA, Canada, Australia, New Zealand and as **an administrative (official)** and **commercial** language in the **Republic of South Africa**, India, the Philippines and the last **British colonies in Africa**. It's important because in **all** the countries that don't speak **English**, it's necessary for working, studying, living and **being** an intelligent person. Because many **English** words are used **by** many people, English is studied as **a** second language, in **all European** schools.

3 WRITING A QUESTIONNAIRE

Hand out photocopies and allow students 10 - 15 minutes to work through sample questionnaires.

Activity 1

Students work in pairs. This activity is designed to get students to think and talk about the usefulness of different types of questionnaire. When pairs have completed tasks 1 - 3, they should form groups of four and compare ideas and sample questions.

Activity 2

In pairs students devise a new questionnaire on one of the suggested subjects. Allow a maximum of 45 minutes for this. Pairs exchange and try out each other's questionnaires, and then, in fours, discuss corrections and improvements. Finally, pairs rewrite questionnaires and try them out on a minimum of ten other people.

4 CONDUCTING AN INTERVIEW

Start with a class discussion: *What are the main differences between questionnaires and interviews as ways of finding out information?*
Discuss the pros and cons of each method. Examples: *Questionnaires are quick to complete, but are impersonal. Interviews are more flexible, but produce less objective information.*
Hand out photocopies and explain *Checklist*. Allow students twenty minutes to work through the three sample checklists.
If time is short you may go straight on to Activity 4.

Activity 1

Pairwork.
Allow students 15 minutes to produce a checklist of main topics for *one* interview.

Activity 2

New pairs - 20 minutes.

Activity 3

New pairs - 25 minutes.

Activity 4

Groups of 4.
Allow thirty minutes for students to prepare and conduct each of their role-play interviews.

5 EXPRESSING INFORMATION IN DIFFERENT WAYS

Explain the aim of this activity to students: to practise different ways of summarising factual information.
Hand out photocopies and allow students twenty minutes to work through the five Examples. Spend ten minutes discussing the relative merits of each Example.

Activities 1 – 4

Students may work uninterrupted through these activities. When they have finished, they should compare results in pairs.

Activity 5

Students write a questionnaire or plan interviews as a means of collecting information. (If they have done Activity 2, Lead-In 3 (page 84), they may use the information from this questionnaire.) Finally they should summarise the information collected, following one of the five Examples.

6 MAKING NOTES

Introduce this activity by asking students how they personally make a written summary of a lecture they are listening to or a textbook they are reading.

Hand out photocopies, and allow students fifteen minutes to read through the three Examples. Discuss the merits of each method.

Activity 1

Students might be expected to highlight the following key points:

Sex equality stops at the front door

MEN are still considered head of the household, but it is women who run the home and do the bulk of the work, according to a survey published today by the Family Policy Studies Centre.

Almost all women – many of whom hold down a job – still do the cleaning, ironing, cooking, shopping, care for the children, and look after elderly relatives. The centre found that, despite the image of the new male who shares the burdens of family responsibility, living examples are hard to find.

Most men are present at the birth of their children and many push the pram, but rearing youngsters remains predominantly a woman's job.

Not surprisingly, women have less spare time than men: seven hours for each weekend day, compared with 10 for men, when working full time. But men do household repairs in three quarters of the homes surveyed.

Activity 2

Students might make notes like this:

Study Plus Centres
1 Forges-les-Eaux
   a in Normandy, near Rouen
   b markets
2 St Valery-sur-Somme
   a small fortress town
   b historical atmosphere
   c coastal town - fishing industry
3 Fougeres
   a military fortress - famous castle
   b agricultural/industrial town
4 St Cast
   a quaint seaside town
   b fishing port
5 Dieppe
   a oldest seaside port - cross Channel ferries
   b lively centre

Activity 3

Students might produce a diagram like this:

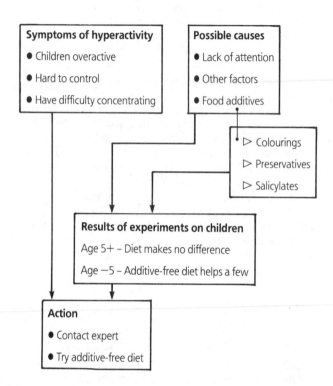

HYPERACTIVE CHILDREN

Students give short talks to their group

7 WRITING LETTERS

Activity 1

Students read the advertisement and the reply. Point out these features of a formal letter:
● The layout: positions of addresses, date, etc.
● Phrases used to begin and end letters
● Key phrase: *I would be grateful if you could . . .*
Students now write a similar letter of their own.

Activity 2

Point out these features:
● Concise statement of intention with place names and dates.
● Key phrases: *Could you possibly . . .* ; *I would be most grateful if you could . . .*
Students write a letter to one of the three Tourist Boards listed. They should mention their own genuine interests if they are going to post their letters.

Activity 3

Point out these key features:
● Writer's statement of intention: *I am writing to invite . . .*
● Details of place, date, subject, audience
● Phrase which reminds reader to reply: *I look forward to hearing from you.*
Students write a similar letter, for example inviting a speaker from the local British Council office.

8 WRITING HEADLINES

Activity 1

Get students to match headlines with beginnings of articles. Check answers: 1F 2A 3B 4D 5G 6C

Activity 2

Students find examples of the ten headline characteristics in the six sample headlines:

1 1	6 3, 4, 5, 6
2 4, 5, 6	7 5
3 1, 5	8 3 (steps up), 4 (wed), 6 (cop)
4 4, 6	9 2 (dad), 4 (copter), 6 (cop)
5 2	10 3 (PM, EEC)

Activity 3

Vocabulary extension

1 PM - Prime Minister
2 EEC - European Economic Community
3 sozzled - drunk
4 cop - policemen
5 copter - helicopter
6 wed - marry

Activity 4

Students may work in pairs.
Remind students to use some of the headline characteristics listed in Activity 2.

Story	Headline idea
1	TITANIC: £30,000 RAISED
2	BERMUDA: WORLD'S "RICHEST PEOPLE"
3	"DOG AND CHIPS PLEASE"
4	PILOTS SACKED AFTER NEAR MISS
5	£12M DRUGS SEIZED
6	20 COWS TO EMIGRATE
7	FOOTBALL "HOOLIGANS" FINED

9 DISCUSSIONS

These activities are intended to prepare students for the various discussions which are essential features of participatory project work. It is important to give students strict deadlines for the different stages of these activities.

Activity 1

Each of the three separate tasks should take five minutes. Finish with class discussion. How much general agreement is there?

Activity 2

Make sure students understand the instructions and allow twenty-five minutes for this activity.

Activity 3

Discuss the problem for a few minutes with the class, and make sure students understand the instructions.

10 USING A DICTIONARY

(*Note:* Many of the 'information gathering' projects suggested in this book involve students in reading difficult authentic texts. Dictionaries are essential tools, and students should learn to use them quickly and accurately. These tasks are designed to help students to get the most out of their dictionaries.)

Activity 1

1 adjective **a./adj**
2 noun **n.**
3 intransitive verb **v.i.**
4 preposition **prep.**
5 conjunction **conj.**
6 countable noun **n.c./n.count**
7 pronoun **pron.**
8 adverb **adv.**

2

Word	Noun	Adjective	Verb	Preposition	Adverb	Conjunction
E.g. fit	✓	✓	✓			
1 half	✓	✓			✓	
2 break	✓		✓			
3 and						✓
4 back	✓	✓	✓		✓	
5 small	✓	✓				
6 well	✓	✓	✓		✓	
7 fine	✓	✓	✓			
8 book	✓		✓			
9 near		✓	✓	✓	✓	
10 while	✓		✓			✓

Activity 2

1 Students check different meanings.
2 1B, 2A, 3A, 4B, 5B

Activity 3

Explain the point of this exercise: to encourage students to use their dictionaries sparingly, and to get used to guessing the meanings of words from their contexts.

Activity 4

- 1 nature
  4 simple
  7 suit
  10 availability
  2 use
  5 operational
  8 humanity
  3 transport
  6 treat
  9 consume

Activity 5

1   1 chimneys   2 shelves
     3 geese   4 monkeys
     5 halves   6 sheep
     7 roofs   8 storeys/stories (U.S.)
     9 mice   10 grouse

2   When used as uncountable nouns, these words refer to substances, materials or unspecified quantities of something (e.g. chicken).
    Countable meanings:
    1 glass — something to drink from
    2 chocolate — small bite-sized or individual sweet made of chocolate
    3 egg — a whole egg including the shell
    4 ice — ice-cream
    5 paper — newspaper
    6 tea — cup of tea
    7 chicken — a whole bird (alive or dead)
    8 iron — implement used for pressing clothes

Activity 6

1   Students check these groups of words and then make sentences to demonstrate their meaning.

2   1 nose   6 blue
     2 read   7 witch
     3 sea   8 lose
     4 would   9 watt
     5 dye   10 wine

Activity 7

Students find the differences in meaning between the two sets of words.

Activity 8

- Meanings:
  1 person or thing that doesn't fit into a group
  2 very rarely, hardly ever
  3 to feel persecuted or inferior
  4 something or someone that you find irritating or annoying
  5 to owe money, especially to the bank
  6 to find just the right words to describe or explain something accurately
  7 a job, occupation
  8 to be reluctant to say directly what you mean
  9 to die
  10 to do something or adjust to something without difficulty

1 GIVING A SHORT TALK

Activity 1

Work in groups of four:

1 Choose **one** of these subjects to talk about:

▷ My family
▷ My best friend
▷ What I do at weekends
▷ The last film I saw
▷ Tourists in my country

▷ My favourite kind of music
▷ Learning English is a waste of time
▷ The importance of money
▷ The worst programme on television
▷ Love

2 Prepare carefully what you are going to say, but do not write your talk in full - you are going to speak not read to your partners
   ▷ First of all write some *headings*. These may be:
   - **Keywords** (Example 1)
   - **Questions and Answers** (Example 2)

Example 1 (Keywords)	Example 2 (Questions and Answers)
The worst programme on television	**The worst programme on television**
1 Dallas	1 What is the worst programme? – *Dallas.*
2 Oil famly	2 What is it about? – *A rich oil family.*
3 Unnatural	3 Why do I dislike Dallas so much? – *It's unnatural.*
4 J. R. Ewing	4 What is worst about Dallas? – *J. R. Ewing.*

3 Now write notes under each heading:

Example 3

The worst programme on television

1 What is the worst programme? – *Dallas.*
   - America's most well-known and longest-running soap opera.
   - Famous for its improbable story.

2 What is it about? – *A rich oil family.*
   - Love, family and business life of the Ewings.
   - Many groups of characters and many sub-plots.

3 Why do I dislike Dallas so much? – *It's unnatural.*
   - Some of the things that happen are really unlikely. For example they bring dead characters back to life.
   - The women are like fashion models or puppets.

4 What is worst about Dallas? – *J. R. Ewing.*
   - He is unbelievably evil: he'd sell his grandmother to make a few dollars.

4 Practise giving your talk (privately) using the notes you have written. Are your notes helpful? If not, rewrite them.

5 Now give the talk to the other students in your group.

Activity 2

For this activity work in pairs.

1 Fill in the spaces in this list of subjects with ideas of your own. (The first two are examples only.)
Do not let your partner see what you are writing.

General subject	Idea for talk
▷ An historical figure: *Gandhi*	
▷ A wild animal: *Tigers*	
▷ A capital city:	
▷ A famous personality:	
▷ A room in the house:	
▷ School life:	
▷ Sport:	

2 Ask your partner which subject he/she would like to give a talk on. Your partner should choose a subject from the general list. Example: *A wild animal*.
Tell your partner: to talk for a minute about e.g. *Tigers*.
Your partner now gives you a subject in the same way.

3 Both of you should prepare and give your talks following the guidelines suggested in Activity 1.

Further activities

● Give a talk about an object, a place, a person or an activity, without mentioning the subject by name.
Other students have to guess the subject. (They can do this during or after the talk.)

● *Work in groups of four.*
Each student writes a single word on a piece of paper and gives it to the student sitting next to him/her.
    In turn, students open their pieces of paper and talk about the word for about a minute without preparation.
    A variation of this has been made into a well-known British radio programme 'Just a Minute'. Here are the rules:

1 During his talk the speaker must not:
    ▷ use the same word more than once (except the word on the paper)
    ▷ hesitate
    ▷ change the subject

2 If the speaker breaks any of these rules, another student can stop him/her, and continue speaking about the same subject for the rest of the minute.

3 The person speaking at the end of one minute wins the game.

2 PROOFREADING: ELEMENTARY

1 Read this short text which contains twenty mistakes:

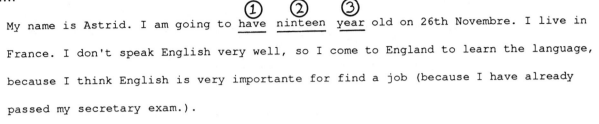

My name is Astrid. I am going to have ninteen year old on 26th Novembre. I live in

France. I don't speak English very well, so I come to England to learn the language,

because I think English is very importante for find a job (because I have already

passed my secretary exam.).

I live on a farme near Ardeligh with an agreeable family and I look for 2 child age

for years old and too years old.

I am here since only six weeks, so I can say much about life in England. For example

the people I meet at the farm are kind and they try to speak me. (The dictionary is

useful also.)

2 Read the text again, underlining and numbering the mistakes.
These are of three different kinds:
● Grammatical ● Spelling ● Choice of words
A mistake of each kind has been marked and corrected for you

3 Now complete this list of corrections:

1 be [Choice of words]..   2 nineteen [Spelling]......   3 years [grammar]......

4 ....   5 ....   6 ....

7 ....   8 ....   9 ....

10 ....   11 ....   12 ....

13 ....   14 ....   15 ....

16 ....   17 ....   18 ....

19 ....   20 ....

4 Now correct this text in the same way:

British Customs and Traditions

Television: Always stupid shows and soop opras. Sometimes there is a good things like the
NEWS.

Eating and Drinking: English people dont say any thing when they starting eating. They have special way
to put froks and the knife after they finished thier meal. They don't drink water and
allways they put a glass of wine in the table.

Shops: Shops usually opening at 9.00 o'clock in the morning and closed at 5.30 in the Eveing
some of shops still open until 8–10 like the big shop. They have a big supermarket
for the thing which is daily use.

PROOFREADING: INTERMEDIATE

1 Read this text which contains many mistakes:

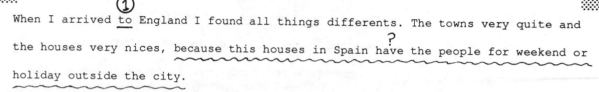

When I arrived ①to England I found all things differents. The towns very quite and the houses very nices, because <u>this houses in Spain have the people for weekend or holiday outside the city.</u> [?]

The food and hours to eat is so different too. Always the english people are very polites, but no really friendly because their are very close into themselves, for that is difficult to made English friends. The English people are very fanatic for themselves, because their thought that they are the best in the world and their county have the best things, so in the other countries there aren't nothing.

2 Read the text again, underlining or numbering mistakes, like the example. Mistakes may be of five kinds:
- Grammatical
- Spelling
- Choice of words
- Word order
- Missing words

3 Write a list of corrections. Example:

1 in [Choice of words]....]

4 Now underline and write a question mark (**?**) above any phrases or sentences which are not clear in meaning. (The first has been marked for you.)

5 Rewrite these phrases or sentences so that they make sense. Example:

? "because people in Spain have houses like these outside the city to visit for holidays or at weekends."

6 Compare and discuss your corrections with a partner.

7 Now correct these texts in the same way:

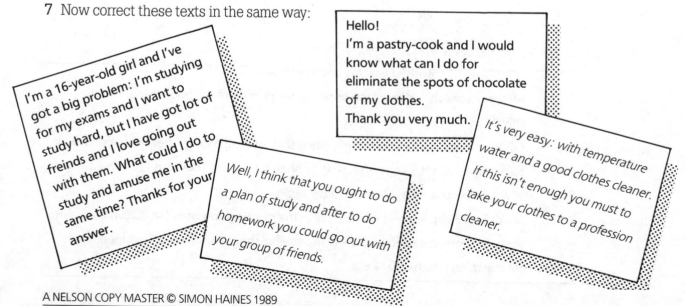

I'm a 16-year-old girl and I've got a big problem: I'm studying for my exams and I want to study hard, but I have got lot of freinds and I love going out with them. What could I do to study and amuse me in the same time? Thanks for your answer.

Well, I think that you ought to do a plan of study and after to do homework you could go out with your group of friends.

Hello!
I'm a pastry-cook and I would know what can I do for eliminate the spots of chocolate of my clothes.
Thank you very much.

It's very easy: with temperature water and a good clothes cleaner. If this isn't enough you must to take your clothes to a profession cleaner.

PROOFREADING: ADVANCED

1 Read through this text quickly to get an idea of what it is about.

At the moment easy communications between countries allow <u>that</u> new habits <u>come in</u> and

relationship between different styles of life. Developing contries depend on developed

countries to progress, and they imitate developed countries like a symbol of progress. It

is a fact that at this moment the Anglo-Saxon civilisation in general, and <u>the United</u>

<u>states to be exact</u>, is identified with the most developed country.

The life in our country Spain like in others appears to be influenced by the

civilization. English language is completely necessary to some jobs, scientific or new

technology vocabulary is full of English words, lot of films are made by English or

American directors, everytime increases the number of multi-nationals in our country,

everytime electoral campeigns seems more american and perhaps everyday we eat more chips

and chicken or hamburgers. Is that a new sign of colonization? Is hamburgers replencing

Spanish food?

2 Read the text again, this time more carefully, underlining any mistakes you can find (words or phrases), and using this system of symbols to identify the type of error:

• Grammar - **G**   • Vocabulary - **V**   • Punctuation - **P**   • Word order - **WO**   • Spelling - **S**   • Missing words - **⋏**

If you do not understand a phrase or sentence, but cannot find any specific mistakes, underline all the words with a wavy line and write **?** in the margin.

3 Work on mistakes one at a time. In the margins, write what you think are the correct words.

4 Compare and discuss your corrections with a partner.

5 Now read and correct the text 'English Language' in the same way:

English Language

English is speaken for more of 350 millions of people and it have got a great

influence in this moment because is considered as the first lenguage in the world. It's

speaked in Great Britain, USA Canada, Australia, New Zealand and as language

administrative and comercial in the South Africa Republic, India, the Philippines and

the last africans colonies of Britain. It's important because in the ever of the

countries that don't speak english, it's necessary for working, studying, living and

been an intelligent person. Because many english words are used for many people.

In the ever of the european schools the English is studied as second language.

3 WRITING A QUESTIONNAIRE

Look at these examples of different questionnaire styles:

• Example 1: Multiple-choice Questions (Factual details)

TELEVISION-WATCHING QUESTIONNAIRE

1 How many hours did you watch TV yesterday?

   a) 6 hours or more . . . . . ☐   b) 4 - 5 hours . . . . ☐

   c) 2 -3 hours . . . . ☐   d) less than 2 hours . . . ☐

2 About how many hours do you watch every week?

   a) more than 40 hours . . . ☐   b) 30 -40 hours . . . . . . ☐

   c) 15 - 30 hours . . . . . . ☐   d) less than 15 hours . . ☐

• Example 2: Multiple-choice Questions (Situational)

SMOKING AND WILLPOWER

You have recently stopped smoking, but you still feel that you would like a cigarette. You are at a party where everyone seems to be smoking. You manage to think about other things until an old friend, who doesn't know you have stopped smoking, offers you a cigarette.

Do you ...

A pretend you haven't stopped and accept the cigarette? . . . . ☐

B admit you have stopped, but take a cigarette and say:

   "Well, just this once."? . . . . ☐

C say you have stopped smoking and refuse the cigarette? . . . . ☐

D say simply: "No thanks, not just now." ? . . . . ☐

● **Example 3: Yes/No Questions**

The George Hotel

Help us to give you a better service

Dear Guest.

We are delighted that you are staying with us and hope that you will feel comfortable in our hotel. We wish to keep up the high standards of service and the friendly atmosphere that The George is famous for. That is why we are asking you to answer a few questions. Please place your completed questionnaire in the envelope and leave it at the reception desk before you leave.

Andrew Hedges
(Manager)

YOUR NAME . . . . .ROOM NUMBER . . . . . .

HOME ADDRESS . . . .

. . . . DATE OF YOUR VISIT . . . .

			Yes	No
1 YOUR ROOM	Did you find your room	clean? _ _ _ _ _ _ _ _ _ _ _ _ _	☐	☐
		comfortable? _ _ _ _ _ _ _ _ _	☐	☐
		pleasant? _ _ _ _ _ _ _ _ _	☐	☐
2 RESTAURANT	Was the waiter polite? _ _ _ _ _ _ _ _ _ _ _ _ _ _ _		☐	☐
	Was the service prompt? _ _ _ _ _ _ _ _ _ _ _ _ _		☐	☐
	Was the quality of the food satisfactory?_ _ _ _ _ _ _ _		☐	☐

● **Example 4: Open-ended Questions**

TEENAGE SMOKING SURVEY

1 How many cigarettes do you smoke a day? · · · · · · · · · · · · · ·

2 How old were you when you had your first cigarette? · · · · · ·

3 Why do you smoke? ·

4 What do you think is the greatest disadvantage of smoking?

· ·

· ·

● Example 5: Ordering

<u>WHY STOP SMOKING?</u>

Put these disadvantages of smoking into what you consider to be their correct order of importance:

A	Smoking makes your clothes smell _	1
B	Smoking is bad for your health _ _ _ _ _ _ _ _ _ _ _ _ _ _ _ _ _ _ _	2
C	Cigarettes are an expensive waste of money _ _ _ _ _ _ _ _ _ _ _	3
D	Smokers can damage the health of non-smokers _ _ _ _ _ _ _ _ _	4
E	Smoking is an anti-social habit _ _ _ _ _ _ _ _ _ _ _ _ _ _ _ _ _	5
F	Smoking causes pollution _	6

(box 5: *C*)

Activity 1

Work in pairs

1 What are the advantages and disadvantages of the different styles of questionnaire? Think and talk about some of these points:

Speed
Efficiency
The type of information needed

What will be done with the results
The number of people to be questioned

2 Which type of questionnaire would you use if you were doing these surveys?

Subject of survey	Type of questionnaire				
	Example:	1	2	3	4	5
1 People's drinking habits					
2 Motorists' knowledge of road safety					
3 People's worst fears and worries					
4 People's reactions to a new food product					
5 People's attitudes towards unemployment					

3 Write one or two sample questions for each of these survey subjects.

Activity 2

Continue working in pairs.

1 Write a questionnaire to find out about **one** of these subjects:

People's use of public transport. (How do people travel? Are they satisfied with the service? etc.)
Young people's future career plans.
People's fears and phobias.

2 Try out your questionnaires on a few people.

3 Make any necessary corrections or improvements to the questions, and try out the revised questionnaire on a larger sample of people.

4 CONDUCTING AN INTERVIEW

If you are conducting an interview, you may work formally through a questionnaire, reading out the questions and noting the answers. Alternatively, you may prefer to work more informally, allowing the person you are interviewing to give more detailed answers than are usually possible if you are working from a questionnaire.

Here are some examples of different types of interview plans:

● **Example 1: Checklist of main topics to be covered in the interview**

```
                        JOB INTERVIEW SHEET
_____

Name: _ _ _ _ _ _ _ _ _ _ _ _ _ _ _ _ _ _ _ _ _ _ _ _ _ _ _ _ _ _ _ _ _
_____

Personal details: _ _ _ _ _ _ _ _ _ _ _ _ _ _ _ _ _ _ _ _ _ _ _ _ _ _ _
_____

Education: _ _ _ _ _ _ _ _ _ _ _ _ _ _ _ _ _ _ _ _ _ _ _ _ _ _ _
_____

Current employment: _ _ _ _ _ _ _ _ _ _ _ _ _ _ _ _ _ _ _ _ _ _ _ _ _
_____

Attitudes: _ _ _ _ _ _ _ _ _ _ _ _ _ _ _ _ _ _ _ _ _ _ _ _ _ _ _
```

● **Example 2: Checklist of main topics + sub-headings**

```
                      TELEVISION-WATCHING HABITS

Name:.......................................................................

Personal details:

Age ..................        Marital Status ............................

Television-watching habits:

    Watching times: .......................................................

    Types of programmes watched: ..........................................

    5 favourite programmes: ...............................................

    Ideas for improvement:  More.............................. programmes

                            Fewer............................. programmes
```

● Example 3: Checklist of main topics + opening questions

```
              ATTITUDES TOWARDS EDUCATION
Own education:
    Could you tell me a little about your own education?
Purposes:
    What, in your opinion, is the main purpose of a state education system?
Ideal school:
    Could you describe the kind of school you would like to send your children to?
```

Activity 1

Work in pairs.

Write a **Checklist of main topics** suitable for an interview in **one** of the following situations (see Example 1):

● You need a new member to join a musical group to which you belong. (The group may be: a pop group/an orchestra/a choir/a jazz group, etc.)

● There is a job vacancy in your office.

Activity 2

Work in pairs.

Write a **Checklist of main topics + sub-headings** suitable for an interview in **one** of these situations (See Example 2):

● You are conducting market research into people's eating habits.

● You are doing a survey of people's tastes in music.

Activity 3

Work in pairs.

Write a **Checklist of main topics + opening questions** suitable for an interview in **one** of these situations (See Example 3):

● You are investigating people's attitudes towards foreigners.

● You are doing research into people's religious beliefs.

Activity 4

Work in groups of 4.

Students 1 and 2

● You have the job of choosing a representative to speak for your class at a forthcoming conference on student rights.

● Write an interview checklist with either sub-headings or opening questions.

● Interview Students 3 and 4 in turn.

● Decide which of the two interviewees will make a better representative.

Students 3 and 4

● You have been short-listed for the job of representing your class at a conference on student rights.

● Prepare for the interview. Think about what qualities the interviewers will look for.

● Before the interviews, decide between yourselves that only **one** of you will give the 'right' answers to the interviewers' questions.

Now swap roles.
This time Students 3 and 4 should interview Students 1 and 2 for:

● Captain of a local sports team *or*

● Secretary of a young people's environmental protection group.

5 EXPRESSING INFORMATION IN DIFFERENT WAYS

Statistical information, collected from questionnaires, interviews or opinion polls, can be processed and expressed in several different ways. Here are some examples:

● **Example 1: Short reports summarising the most important information:**

A report published last week shows that more British families than ever before are going abroad for their summer holidays.

Spain is still the most popular holiday country: last year 52% of British tourists spent one or two weeks at a resort on the Costa Brava. Of this 52%, more than three-quarters had bought a package holiday from one of the major British travel companies. Only one family in twenty drove to Spain in their own car.

It is also clear from the report that many families are getting tired of Spain and want a change. The second most popular tourist country was Greece: 26% of families questioned spent their last summer holidays on one of the Greek islands.

When asked why they went abroad for their holidays, 90% gave 'good weather' as their main reason. Another 7% said they went for the food and drink, but only 2% mentioned 'meeting different people' or 'finding out about other cultures' as their main reason.

One fifth of the people interviewed had two foreign holidays last year.

● **Example 2: Statistics summarised in tables of figures**

THE GREAT DIVIDE: How we spend our money

LOW INCOME

BOTTOM 20%
% of spending
Housing 23
Fuel 12
Food 25
Drink &
Tobacco 7
Clothes 5
Household
goods 12
Transport 6
Services
& misc. 10

MIDDLE INCOME

MIDDLE 60%
% of spending
Housing 17
Fuel 7
Food 22
Drink &
Tobacco 8
Clothes 7
Household
goods 14
Transport 15
Services
& misc. 10

HIGH INCOME

TOP 20%
% of spending
Housing 15
Fuel 5
Food 18
Drink &
Tobacco 7
Clothes 8
Household
goods 16
Transport 17
Services
& misc. 14

● **Example 3: Bar charts**

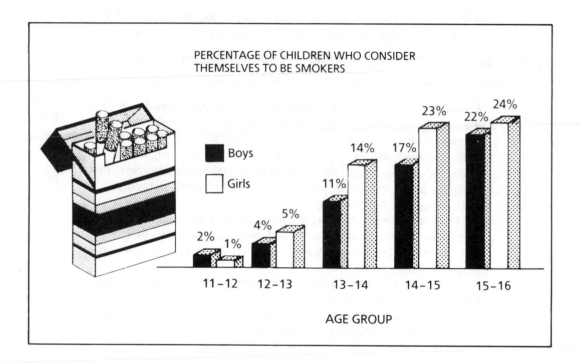

● **Example 4: Graphs**

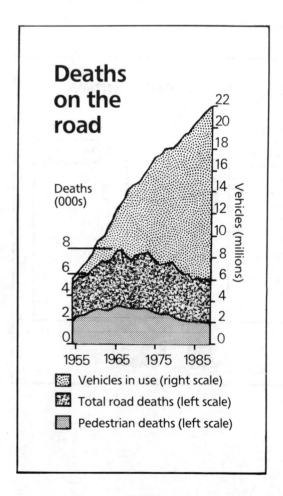

● **Example 5: Pie charts**

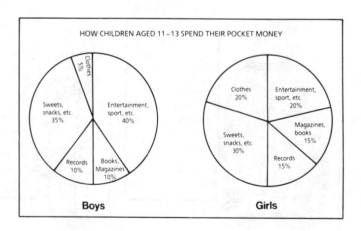

Activity 1

Write a short report, like Example 1, summarising the most important information included in **one** of the following:

▷ The Great Divide: How we spend our money (Example 2).

▷ Percentage of children who consider themselves to be smokers (Example 3).

▷ How children spend their pocket money (Example 5).

Activity 2

▷ Draw a Pie Chart, like Example 5, to show how Middle Income Earners spend their money (see Example 2).

Activity 3

▷ Draw a Graph, like Example 4, to show how the percentage of boys who smoke and drink increases between the ages of 11 and 16 (Example 3).

Activity 4

▷ Draw a Bar Chart, like Example 3, comparing the percentage of income spent by the three income groups on Housing and Food (Example 2).

Activity 5

Work in pairs.

▷ Write a questionnaire or conduct interviews to find out
  either:
  ● What the other students in your class do in their spare time.
  or
  ● How the other students in your class earn and spend their money.

▷ Carry out the survey

▷ Summarise the results of your survey in as many different ways as you can, using Examples 1-5 as models.

▷ Finally, discuss which is the most suitable way of expressing the results of your survey.

6 MAKING NOTES

Making notes on a written text or a talk is an activity which people do in many different ways - there is no one correct method. What is important is that the note-writer is able to summarise key points quickly and then understand at a later time what he/she has written.

Here are some examples of different styles of note-making.

Example 1: Highlighting points in the text:

This method is simple and quick, and suitable for short texts. The underlined or highlighted words and phrases remind you at a glance of the main points of what you have read.

DRUNK DRIVERS' —NAMES ON TV—

Each year 250 people are killed on the roads of Scotland, and alcohol-related accidents are costing Scottish taxpayers £100 million annually. But, starting next week, television viewers in Scotland will see a list of the names and addresses of motorists who have been convicted of drunken driving. Naming offenders is part of a Scottish Television campaign against drinking and driving.

In another programme, the parents of children who have been killed by drunken drivers will talk about how their lives have been ruined. And a driver who seriously injured a 13-year-old boy will describe the feelings of guilt that will remain with him for the rest of his life.

Two separate campaigns to fight against under-age drinking and drunk-driving are being organised by beer companies, pub owners, and supermarkets.

All these campaigns have the enthusiastic support of Scottish police and doctors.

● Example 2: Headings and sub-headings:

This method takes time and thought, but is more suitable for longer texts, chapters of books, etc.

Notice these points:

- the use of a systematic numbering system.
- the use of headings and sub-headings.
- the lack of unnecessary words, for example, articles (*a/the/this*, etc.).
- the few verbs that are used are in the infinitive or imperative forms.

SPEAK UP FOR YOURSELF!

At some time most people are called upon to speak out in public, whether formally or informally, and though the prospect may seem terrifying there are simple ways to overcome the tremors . . .

● **Be Yourself:** Imitating someone else's style will sound ridiculous – after all it's *you* they asked to speak.

● **Be Heard:** Wait until the audience is quiet before beginning.

● **Be Relevant:** Cut out waffle and don't introduce anecdotes out of context. Be punchy and precise – leave them wanting more rather than less.

● **Be Prepared:** Readiness is the key to success; don't be fooled by 'off-the-cuff' speakers, they've probably spent a lifetime rehearsing 'spontaneity'.

Steer clear of controversy – e.g. former lovers at a wedding reception, or politics and religion.

'In-jokes' are boring for everyone else and avoid repeating words by finding alternatives in a dictionary.

Arrange your material by jotting down headings and phrases on plain postcards or index cards and using different coloured pens. These reminders allow you to look up at the audience for most of your speech.

NO BOOZE!

Underline names and dates – you may think you know them, but you might not on the day. Thread the cards together with string; loose ones get muddled or dropped!

Relax and smile but refuse the Dutch courage of alcohol – it slurs words.

Occasionally, it's necessary to speak unprepared – in an emergency for example. Keep calm – taking two deep breaths really does help – and avoid panic. Asking people to move towards the exit achieves more than screaming 'fire!' for instance.

Notes

GIVING A TALK
1 Ways to get over fear
 a Be yourself - relax/smile.
 b Wait for silence.
 c Keep to point - not too much.
 d Prepare well-written notes.

2 What to avoid
 a Controversy.
 b In-jokes.
 c Alcoholic drinks.

Example 3: Diagrammatic notes:

This method is particularly useful for making notes on texts which contain ideas rather than simple facts. Its effectiveness is due largely to its visual impact, which allows the relationships between ideas to be clearly shown and is an aid to the note-maker's memory.

THE PRICE OF MEAT THESE DAYS IS SHEER MURDER

Murderously expensive

The reasons are obvious. In Britain only a small proportion of the feed required for animals is actually grown and the remainder must therefore be imported – at a phenomenal cost to the meat farmer and to the country's Balance of Payments.

Intensive farming methods mean that increased fuel charges also affect the many meat farmers who now rear their animals indoors. Such unnatural conditions will inevitably lead to disease if not controlled with drugs, and vet's bills can be considerable. Transportation, too, is becoming increasingly costly.

All these charges must be passed on to the consumer if the meat farmer is to stay in business. What's more, the British tax payer pays not once, but twice for his meat. He pays the second time through subsidies and compensation granted by the government to prop up what is undoubtedly a dying business.

Murderously wasteful

One third of the world's population is starving, yet this planet can supply ample food to feed everyone. The wastage occurs because valuable, protein-rich plant food is fed to meat producing animals instead of to humans – and its a wastage that is multiplied incredibly when we calculate what we get back in return.

An average of 90% of the protein in the original plant food is used by the animals for growth, leaving only 10% for those who eat their flesh. Feeding plant foods to meat-producing animals is like throwing them away, yet these nourishing foods could literally mean the difference between life and death to millions of people.

Diagrammatic notes:

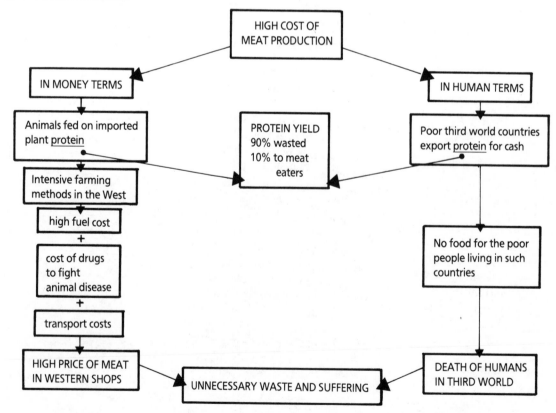

Activity 1

- Read this newspaper article and highlight or underline the key points, as in Example 1.

Sex equality stops at the front door

MEN are still considered head of the household, but it is women who run the home and do the bulk of the work, according to a survey published today by the Family Policy Studies Centre.

Almost all women – many of whom hold down a job – still do the cleaning, ironing, cooking, shopping, care for the children, and look after elderly relatives. The centre found that, despite the image of the new male who shares the burdens of family responsibility, living examples are hard to find.

Most men are present at the birth of their children and many push the pram, but rearing youngsters remains predominantly a woman's job.

Not surprisingly, women have less spare time than men: seven hours for each weekend day, compared with 10 for men, when working full time. But men do household repairs in three quarters of the homes surveyed.

- Now copy the highlighted or underlined words and phrases on to a piece of paper, and without looking at the original text, write your own summary of the story.

Activity 2

- A friend has asked you to find out about Study Plus French Language Holidays. Read this advertisement which you find in a magazine in your local library.
- Now read the text again and make notes to remind you of information you think your friend will want to know. Use headings and sub-headings, as in Example 2.

Fougères

OUR CENTRES

Forges-les-Eaux

This delightful Norman country market town is less than an hour's drive from Rouen. There are many typically French sights and activities here, such as the old fashioned animal and shopping markets in the main square in front of the Hôtel de Ville, which is also worth a visit for some French conversation and a good local atmosphere.

St. Valéry-sur-Somme

A tiny fortress town in a superb situation on the estuary of the River Somme, with all the attributes we think are necessary for a successful course – providing a fascinating and historic atmosphere, a thriving fishing industry, which is a traditional employment here and, most of all, the unspoilt everyday pace of a typical French coastal town.

Fougères

This was an important military fortress in the Middle Ages, and the existing castle is one of the most famous in France.

Fougères is an important agricultural and industrial town and local granite is used by stone masons throughout the country. Timber from the nearby forest was used for clogs until 1952, but now local crafts include wood sculpture, weaving, pottery, wrought iron work and tanning, providing an emphasis which will enable this course to be right on target for language-based TVEI or CPVE work.

St. Cast

St. Cast is a quaint seaside resort which is similar to a picturesque Cornish fishing village, with six bays of soft sand which are sheltered by the cliffs and background hills.

Because the town is a fishing port it provides wonderful conversation pieces and the addition of a good selection of shops in the winding main street will provide a never-ending stream of situations for developing proficient conversation.

Dieppe

The oldest French seaside port, now a major terminal for cross Channel ferries. The bustle of this port town and the activity during the main holiday season makes it a lively centre for the course venue. There will be a wide range of topics available for study and students will find it hard to be bored during the busy days.

Activity 3

- You have to give a short talk to your class about the relationship between food additives and hyperactivity in children. Read this short text about this relationship:

HYPERACTIVITY IN CHILDREN

In the early 1970s an American doctor claimed that many over-active children who were difficult to control and who found it hard to concentrate could be cured if they ate a diet free from added colours, preservatives and salicylates. (Salicylates are naturally-occurring compounds in apples, oranges, tomatoes, berries and other fruits.)

When the diet was assessed objectively, it was found to be ineffective. Some of the children did improve, but the cause was thought to be the much greater amount of attention they were given, not the diet. However, there is some evidence that a very small number of children under five years may be particularly sensitive to certain additives and benefit from an additive-free diet. But a great many other factors besides additives also cause problems for these children.

If you suspect that a child is hyperactive, it is crucial that expert diagnosis be sought.

- Make diagrammatic notes on the text, as in Example 3.
- Using only your diagram, write out or give your short talk.

7 WRITING LETTERS

Activity 1

Letters in reply to advertisements

1 Read this advertisement, and the letter which was written in reply to it:

PEN PALS

A monthly catalogue of penfriends and **EXCITING NEW CONTACTS** locally, nationwide and in distant lands.

Every page is **ABSOLUTELY PACKED** with descriptive commentaries and photographs of people from all walks of life.

WRITE NOW enclosing a stamp, if possible. By return of post we will **RUSH** to you an **APPROVAL** copy of our catalogue to view for yourself.

THE PEN SOCIETY, Dept. H.34 Chorley, Lancs. PR7 4BS.

The Pen Society,
Dept, H,34<
Chorley,
Lancs PR7 4BS

16, The Chase,
West Sudbury,
Suffolk IP8 7QP

18.8.88

Dear Sir,

    I have just seen your advertisement in this month's issue of Company magazine. I have wanted a penfriend for some time, but I didn't know who to contact. I see from your advertisement that I could write to someone in this country or abroad.

    I would be very grateful if you could send me a copy of your catalogue. I am enclosing a stamp.

    Yours faithfully,

Christine Fenn

---

2 Now write a similar letter in reply to one of these advertisements.

MEET PEOPLE AND TRAVEL!
Train for a Fun Career at the
HOTEL CAREER CENTRE

10 and 5 week Reception Courses
(includes Computers & Typing)

16 week course in Reception,
Housekeeping and Food Service.

1 year General Hotel Diploma Course.

11 week Cookery Certificate Course.

Excellent Job-Finder Service.
Accommodation arranged.
Write or phone for free details.

**Hotel Career Centre
43 Norwich Avenue West,
Bournemouth, Dorset.
Tel: (0202) 291877**

Express Yourself...
Bring Out Your Creativity...
Earn Fees and Royalties...

SUCCESSFUL WRITERS

Enjoy the experience of others reading your work and of receiving really worthwhile income. Short stories, articles, novels, plays, TV and radio scripts, even poetry, are covered by our courses which have helped many fulfil themselves by getting into print.
Achieve Your Writing Ambition
Whatever your writing ambition, we and our qualified tutors will guide you as you study in the comfort of your own home.... at your own speed. Develop the facility to write as you want and help satisfy the demand from editors always hungry for fresh talent.

Unlimited, No-Risk Guarantee
The Course comes with the guarantee of unlimited tuition. And if you have not learned enough from your writing to pay the fees by the time you complete it, we will refund your money. We are, incidentally, an accredited correspondence college. Examine the Course for 21 days without obligation. But first send for our....

Free Book
Intriguing as its title 'Write Right' is a valuable hardback, desk side book. Apply for details within 7 days and it is yours to keep whatever you decide.

CACC Call us now, free of charge
dial 100 and ask for
'Freefone Successful Writers'
or simply write to
Successful Writers, FREEPOST TNS 501 Newton Abbot, Devon, TQ12 1BR
(no stamp required),

Activity 2

Letters requesting information

1 Read this letter requesting tourist information:

Southern Tourist Board
Town Hall Centre,
Leigh Road,
Eastliegh,
Hants, Great Britain SO5 4DE

35, Cours Lafayette,
69006 Lyon,
France

14th September 1988

Dear Sir,

I am planning a camping holiday in England next summer. I shall be arriving in Southampton and would like to spend the first week of my stay in the New Forest. Could you possibly send me some general information about your region and a list of campsites in the New Forest area.

While I am in England I would also like to go to a folk music festival, so I would be most grateful if you could send me details of any festivals that are taking place in your area between June 22nd and July 13th.

Yours faithfully

Jean Blanc

Jean Blanc

2 Write a similar letter requesting information about one of these places in Britain:

Places	When	Interests	Tourist Board address
Dartmoor	July 1–15	Horse-riding	West Country Tourist Board, Trinity Court, 37 Southernhay East, Exeter EX1 1QS
Norfolk Broads	Sept 6–23	Sailing	East Anglia Tourist Board, 14 Museum Street, Ipswich IP1 1HU
Lake District	May 10–31	Walking/Climbing	Cumbria Tourist Board, Ashleigh, Holly Road, Windermere, Cumbria LA23 2AG

Activity 3

Letters of invitation

1 Read this letter:

The Park School,
Summerwell Avenue, Cambridge CB2 1JY

Oxfam,
Education Department,
274, Banbury Road
Oxford OX2 7DX

17th May 1988

Dear Sir,

I am writing to invite an Oxfam representative to speak at our annual Sixth Form Conference which is being held at the Park School on September 17th.

The subject of this year's conference is Third World Poverty. We have also invited Population Concern to send a speaker.

The day's programme has not yet been finalised, but we should be able to send you full details before the end of June. We intend to charge a £2 conference fee, and will be donating all the money collected to Oxfam and Population Concern.

I look forward to hearing from you.

Yours faithfully

James Edwards.

James Edwards (Headteacher)

---

2 Write a letter to an organisation in your country, inviting them to send a speaker to a meeting at your school.

8 WRITING HEADLINES

Activity 1

Match headlines 1-6 with the correct newspaper stories A - G.
One story has no headline.

1 ▷ **I'VE LOST TWO STONE FOR ANDREW SAYS FERGIE**

2 ▷ *PM steps up attack on EEC 'state'*

3 ▷ **Learn to spell rite, dad**

4 ▷ **Copter crash couple to wed**

5 ▷ Gas 'pumped into burning oil platform'

6 ▷ *Sozzled society girl drove past cop*

A ▼

CHILDREN set a spelling test for adults and discovered their elders were not necessarily their betters.

MRS THATCHER yesterday stepped up her personal crusade against any trend towards a federal united Europe yesterday, predicting that "a centralised government in Europe would be a nightmare".

▲ B

C

A HIGH society writer had drunk more than twice the limit when she zoomed past a policeman trying to flag her car down.
Tanya Kindersley, great niece of former Bank of England director Lord Kindersley, was fined £250 and banned for 18 months yesterday.

D ▶ TV presenters Mike Smith and Sarah Greene, who almost died in a helicopter crash three weeks ago, are to marry.
Mike proposed as the couple recovered in hospital from the serious injuries they suffered when their copter plunged to the ground.

FERGIE says she has lost an astonishing two stone since she gave birth **F ▶** to baby Bea - and it's all for Andrew.

E ▶ Two airmen were killed last night when their RAF Phantom jet crashed near Abingdon, Oxfordshire, during a training exercise for today's Battle of Britain open day.

New questions about the unexpected intensity of the fires on the Piper Alpha oil platform, which killed 167 people two months ago, were raised last night by the Labour MP, Mr Frank Doran. ◀ **G**

Activity 2

A good headline makes you want to read the article that follows it.

Here are some of the ways in which they attract the readers' attention:

1 They use the names of famous people.
2 They use sensational words or slang.
3 They use words that someone has spoken.
4 They use words in interesting-sounding combinations.
5 They make a joke with words.

Here are some of the ways in which they save space:

6 They leave out articles ('the' 'a/an' etc.).
7 They leave our parts of verbs (e.g. auxiliaries).
8 They use special 'newspaper jargon'.
9 They use shortened words.
10 They use abbreviations.

• Find examples of these ten features in the six headlines.

Activity 3

● Read the newspaper stories A - G and then guess the meanings of these words:

1 PM ....   2 EEC ....

3 sozzled ....   4 cop ....

5 copter ....   6 wed ....

Activity 4

● Make up headlines for these news stories:

1 ....

....

The youngest survivor of the Titanic was present yesterday as more than £30,000 was raised at an auction to mark the 76th anniversary of the disaster.

2 ....

....

The 56,000 residents of Bermuda were the world's richest in 1986, with an average income of $20,420 a year, the World Bank reported. The Swiss were the next highest, with average incomes of $17,840, while US citizens were third, with $17,500.

3 ....

....

Calcutta has offered to sell dogs to South Korea where they are part of most people's diet.
There are more than 100,000 ownerless dogs in Calcutta.

4 ....

....

Two airline pilots have lost their jobs after a landing error at Gatwick airport which brought two planes carrying 225 people close to a head-on collision.

5 ....

....

Customs officers at Heathrow Airport seized 90 kilos of cocaine with a street value of £12 million yesterday.

6 ....

....

At least 20 British cows will shortly be leaving the country by plane for a new life in the Mukono area of Uganda. Awaiting each of them is a poor peasant farmer and two acres of elephant grass.

7 ....

....

Two England and Rangers footballers were fined for fighting during the match between Rangers and Celtic in October.

9 DISCUSSIONS

Activity 1

Coming to an agreement

Two Weeks in London

You are going on a two-week school trip to London. You can take ten things with you in addition to your clothes and washing things.

Task 1 (Individuals):   Write a list of the ten things you would like to take. (You have five minutes to write your list.)

Task 2 (Pairs):   Now compare your list with another student, and agree on a new list of the five most important things to take. (You have five minutes to reach an agreement.)

Task 3 (Groups of 4):   You and your partner now join another pair of students and compare your lists of five things. This time you have to agree on the three most important things to take to London. (Again, you have five minutes to reach an agreement.)

Activity 2

Allocating tasks

Sharing a Holiday Flat

You and three friends are going on holiday together. You have agreed to share a flat.

Task 1 (Groups of 4):   Discuss and make a list of the jobs that will have to be done around the flat to ensure that the holiday is enjoyable. Examples: cooking/cleaning/shopping, etc.

Task 2 (Individuals):   Each student writes a list of three different jobs that he or she is good at, or would like to do during the holiday.

Task 3 (Groups of 4):   Finally, all four students compare lists and decide who is going to do which job. (You have ten minutes to allocate the jobs.)

Activity 3

Discussing a plan of action

Getting Home

You and three friends have spent the weekend at a pop music festival several hundred kilometres away from where you live. It is now Sunday afternoon, and you have just discovered that all your personal belongings have been stolen from your tent. You have lost your train tickets and most of your money. (In any case, you have already missed the last train home.)

Task 1 (Individuals):   Each student works out an individual plan of action. Think about some of these points:
▷ getting your belongings back
▷ getting home
▷ letting people at home know what is happening
Write down your plan of action: what you would do first, second, third, etc.

Task 2 (Groups of 4):   Now, discuss your plan with your friends. (You have ten minutes to come to an agreement on a plan of action.)

10 USING A DICTIONARY

Activity 1

1 Look at the introduction to your English dictionary and make a note of the abbreviations used for these 'parts of speech' or grammar words:

1 adjective .... 2 noun ....

3 intransitive verb .... 4 preposition ....

5 conjunction .... 6 countable noun ....

7 pronoun .... 8 adverb ....

2 Now look up in your dictionary the words in the table and tick the appropriate columns of parts of speech (many of the words can be used in more than one way).

Word	Noun	Adjective	Verb	Preposition	Adverb	Conjunction
E.g. fit	✔	✔	✔			
1 half						
2 break						
3 and						
4 back						
5 small						
6 well						
7 fine						
8 book						
9 near						
0 while						

Activity 2

1 Use your dictionary to check the different meanings of these words:

1 A plain (noun) ....

  B plain (adjective) ....

2 A post (verb) ....

  B post (noun) ....

3 A last (adjective) ....

  B last (verb) ....

4 A bend (noun) ....

  B bend (verb) ....

5 A staple (noun) ....

  B staple (adjective) ....

2 The same five words are used in the following sentences. Decide whether they are like A or B.

1 I can't stand **plain** ice-cream. It's absolutely tasteless ....☐

2 You did remember to **post** my letter, didn't you? ....☐

3 Where did you go for your holiday **last** year? ....☐

4 Yuri Geller says he can **bend** spoons ....☐

5 Rice is the **staple** diet in China ....☐

Activity 3

1 Underline all the words in this text that you do not understand.

> Man cannot live without water and early settlements were always close to natural supplies of water such as streams and rivers. With the great increase in population over the centuries and the need for man to spread himself over the land, he has devised means of carrying water to where he needs it – an early example of this was the Roman aqueduct. The use of water and its transportation has been developed over the years until today, when most of us simply turn on a tap in our own homes and the water flows. Behind this simple operation has been built a vast network of pumphouses, treatment works, laboratories, reservoirs and pipes to ensure that a supply of water suitable for human consumption is always available at the turn of a tap.

2 Make a list of **half** of the words you have underlined and look up their meanings in a dictionary.

3 Now guess the meanings of the other half of the words you underlined in the text.

4 Finally compare your guesses with a partner before checking the meanings in your dictionary.

Activity 4

Use your dictionary to find words related to these words from the text.

E.g. settlement - *verb:* settle ....

1 natural - *noun:* ....
2 use - *verb:* ....
3 transportation - *verb:* ....
4 simply - *adjective:* ....
5 operation - *adjective:* ....

6 treatment - *verb:* ....
7 suitable - *verb:* ....
8 human - *noun:* ....
9 consumption - *verb:* ....
10 available - *noun:* ....

Activity 5

1 Use your dictionary to check the plural forms of these nouns:

1 chimney ....
3 goose ....
5 half ....
7 roof ....
9 mouse ....

2 shelf ....
4 monkey ....
6 sheep ....
8 storey ....
10 grouse ....

2 What is the difference in meaning between the countable and uncountable form of these words:

Word	Uncountable meaning	Countable meaning
1 glass	....	....
2 chocolate	....	....
3 egg	....	....
4 ice	....	....
5 paper	....	....
6 tea	....	....
7 chicken	....	....
8 iron	....	....

Activity 6

1 Use your dictionary to check the difference in meaning between these sets of words:

    1 scream/shout/cry (verbs)
    2 cut/bruise/injury (nouns)
    3 pleasant/pretty/tasty (adjectives)
    4 flame/fire/smoke (nouns)
    5 worried/upset/nervous (adjectives)

2 Think of other words in English which sound like these words but have a different spelling. If you are in doubt, check the pronunciation in your dictionary:

1 knows .... 2 reed ....

3 see .... 4 wood ....

5 die .... 6 blew ....

7 which .... 8 loos ....

9 what .... 10 whine ....

Activity 7

1 Check the difference in meaning between these pairs of phrasal verbs:

1 break up .... / break down ....

2 put off .... / put on ....

3 do up .... / do out ....

4 give away .... / give in ....

5 get on with .... / get on to ....

2 Check the difference in meaning between these pairs of verbs:

1 set up .... / upset ....

2 take over .... / overtake ....

3 do out .... / outdo ....

4 set off .... / offset ....

5 run out (of) .... / outrun ....

Activity 8

- Use your dictionary to find the meanings of these idiomatic phrases. (If you do not find the phrases under the first headword, try one of the other words in the phrase.)

1 the odd man out ....

2 once in a blue moon ....

3 to have a chip on one's shoulder ....

4 a pain in the neck ....

5 to be in the red ....

6 to hit the nail on the head ....

7 a walk of life ....

8 to beat about the bush ....

9 to kick the bucket ....

10 to take something in one's stride ....

APPENDIX

The following is a list of Tourist Boards:

English Tourist Board
Thames Tower
Blacks Road
Hammersmith
London W6 9EL
Tel: 01-846 9000

Regional tourist boards

Cumbria Tourist Board
Ashleigh
Holly Road
Windermere
Cumbria LA23 2AG
Tel: 09662 4041

East Anglia Tourist Board
14 Museum Street
Ipswich
IP1 1HU
Tel: 0473 214211

East Midlands Tourist Board
Exchequergate
Lincoln
LN2 1PZ
Tel: 0522 31521

Heart of England Tourist Board
P.O. Box 15
Worcester
WR1 2JT
Tel: 0905 29299

London Visitor and Convention Bureau
26 Grosvenor Gardens
London
SW1W 0DU
Tel: 01-730 3450

Northumbria Tourist Board
9 Osborne Terrace
Jesmond
Newcastle-upon-Tyne
Tel: 0632 816624

North West Tourist Board
Last Drop Village
Bromley Cross
Bolton
BL7 9PZ
Tel: 0204 593759

Southern Tourist Board
Town Hall Centre
Leigh Road
Eastleigh
SO5 4DE
Tel: 0703 611248

South East English Tourist Board
Cheviot House
4-6 Monson Road
Tunbridge Wells
TN1 1NH
Tel: 0892 36381

Thames and Chilterns Tourist Board
8 The Market Place
Abingdon
OX14 3UD
Tel: 0235 30649

West Country Tourist Board
Trinity Court
37 Southernhay East
Exeter
EX1 1QS
Tel: 0392 76351

Yorkshire and Humberside Tourist Board
312 Tadcaster Road
York
YO2 2HF
Tel: 0904 7077225

Other tourist committees

**Isle of Man
Tourist Board**
13 Victoria Street
Douglas
Isle of Man
Tel: 0624 4323

**Scottish
Tourist Board**
23 Ravelston Terrace
Edinburgh
EH4 3EU
Tel: 031-332 2433

**Northern Ireland
Tourist Board**
River House
48 High Street
Belfast
BT1 2DS
Tel: 0232 31221

**Wales
Tourist Board**
Brunel House
2 Fitzalan Road
Cardiff
CF2 1UY
Tel: 0222 499909